INNER♥VIEWS

Stories on the Strength of America

Julie Madsen, Ph.D.

with
Bruce Madsen, photojournalist

Quixote Publications
Berea, Ohio

Copyright ©2000
Self Expression News Service, Inc.
Printed in the United States of America.
All rights reserved.
ISBN 0-9633083-9-4

Quixote Publications
490 Merrimak Drive
Berea, Ohio 44017-2241

First edition
10 9 8 7 6 5 4 3 2 1

Library of Congress Cataloging-in-Publication Data

Madsen, Julie, 1947-
    Inner views : stories on the strength of America / by Julie Madsen, with Bruce Madsen, photojournalist. -- 1st ed.
    p.   cm.
    ISBN 0-9633083-9-4
    1. Conduct of life Case studies. 2. United States Biography.
I. Madsen, Bruce, 1944- .   II. Title
    BJ1547.4.M25   1999   99-37779
    158' .0973--dc21   CIP

Quotations from Henry David Thoreau in Chapter 4 are from his essays, "Walking" (1862) and "Life Without Principle" (1863).

Cover photo by Bruce Madsen
Mount Rainier, State of Washington

Contents

Acknowledgments

This book is dedicated to those who believe that stories of goodness and hope are beneficial to one's mental and spiritual health. These persons have been our ordinary heroes: Mary Jane Skala, editor of *The Sun Press* of a newspaper chain in northeast Ohio, who took a leap of faith when she hired two wannabe weekly columnists and who so graciously edited our manuscript; Julie's parents, Ron and Betty Schumaker, who gathered, sorted, and sent our mail to post offices across America; Bruce's parents, Billie and Lincoln Madsen, long-time RV adventurers, who gave continuous on-the-road advice; Pat Mote of Quixote Publications, who followed our journey through the *Sun* newspaper columns and called to ask to publish the book—what a godsend she has been. And we are especially grateful to all the friends and perfect strangers who offered their hospitality and heartwarming stories to make this book and this dream possible.

We also acknowledge those world-famous teachers whose lives and whose deaths in 1997 inspired our journey of hope. These are extraordinary heroes. Veteran CBS newsman Charles Kuralt died on July 4. He chronicled rare Americans and unlikely heroes and inspired our decision to hit the road in search of upbeat news. While looking down from an airplane at night at twinkling city lights, Kuralt once said, "Each light is a story."

We honor the lessons of Mother Teresa who comforted the dying, the hopeless, and the orphaned. She taught us how to love. Mother Teresa will be remembered as the tiny nun with Michael-the-archangel wings, battling poverty on all levels, knowing that "the greatest poverty is to feel unwanted and unloved."

And Victor Frankl, the Austrian psychiatrist, concentration camp survivor, and author of *Man's Search for Meaning*, will live forever in our hearts. When the world was full of darkness, Frankl delivered hope. "There is nothing in the world that would so effectively help one to survive even the worst conditions as the knowledge that there is a meaning in one's life," he wrote.

Ordinary and extraordinary heroes carry the same message—that hope is not just wishful thinking, but a living expression of faith, confidence, love, and endurance. By their lives, our lives are richer. By their guidance, our hearts are more tender. By their message, our connection feels closer to each other and to God.

The Madsens

February 1999

Introduction

It felt like destiny that Bruce and I met over blueberry muffins and spicy hot wings at a potluck dinner for singles. Nine months later we exchanged "I do's," followed by a potluck wedding feast. But after two years of hectic professional schedules, we did some soul searching. Was our life together meant to be about re-roofing, resurfacing the driveway, and redecorating the house? Surely, it was time to revamp and rethink our dreams.

At forty-seven, I was less and less willing to sit still in my beige-walled psychology practice. Was this what having a Ph.D. was all about? And Bruce, age fifty, a Stanford grad who'd worked twenty-six years for General Electric, longed to be with people, not computers. Somehow, we knew that tossing high-paying careers to the wind wouldn't fly unless we balanced our losses with a lifestyle that offered, paradoxically, more for less—more self-expression, more adventure, more time together, less expense, less maintenance, and less stuff.

One evening in November, I came home from a typical ten-hour day, plopped face-up on the bed, glared at the blank white ceiling, and announced, "This can't be my life."

"What would you rather be doing?" Bruce asked.

Just as spring flowers thrust through winter's cold ground, the words popped right out. "Writing uplifting stories of hope," I said.

Four months later we quit our jobs, put our sprawling Shaker Heights, Ohio, house up for sale, and sold all the things we loved—fine china, antique furniture, oriental rugs, and compact cars. In a moment of truth, we traded the worn-out dream of riches and professional security for a life of adventure and the uncertainty of the open road.

Our grown children thought we were nuts, but most of our baby-booming cronies wanted to come along. It was risky business, but we had a cause: Under the guise of "Bounty Hunters," (bounty means goodness) we would sniff out stories of courage, faith, and hope—in spite of what we heard and saw on the nightly news.

Our spirited decision was not without anxiety. Bruce's last day of work, January 6, 1995, was mixed with joy and quiet terror. What if the house doesn't sell? Could we master towing a rig, changing careers, and adjusting to a new lifestyle all at once? Had we overestimated our human powers, or simply lost our marbles?

In mid-January we went to Cleveland's annual RV show and jumped right into the sea of travel trailers, fifth wheels, and motor homes. After wading through row after row of high-tech, low-maintenance mobile units, we chose the sensible travel trailer. In March, our shiny home-on-wheels was delivered from the manufacturer in Indiana to the dealer in Ohio. Bruce was like a kid turned loose in an amusement park—no bars held, teeming with the spirit of adventure.

Then—wham. The week before we left Ohio, tragic news shattered the nation. The Oklahoma City Federal Building was bombed. Thus, we dedicated our odyssey to the end of violence. In the middle of utter despair, we launched a journey of hope.

Not knowing where or how to begin, we decided to make a trial run. Two days later, we landed at Pride RV Resort in Maggie Valley, North Carolina, where we hosted our first official potluck dinner. Fellow campers, all strangers, brought covered dishes and heartfelt stories. The clubhouse was packed full. Then on May 17, while we were camped in Tallulah Falls, Georgia, *USA Today* ran a story about our departure: "Have RV, will travel in search of an amiable America." The stories came rolling in from around the country. We returned to Cleveland for two weeks to share the good news, then headed west across America.

The stories you are about to read are grouped into categories rather than in the order in which we gathered them. This adventure that zigzagged the U.S. and covered all fifty states has been more than a happy trail. It has become a sacred journey. Thanks for coming along.

Brotherly Love

Disillusioned by the nightly news and haunted by the question, "Is America a hopeless, dangerous place?"—we left our professional jobs and suburban security for a life of adventure on the open road. We were guided by a deep desire to know how people find meaning in their lives—especially when surrounded by adversity, confusion, and growing public cynicism.

As we traveled over bumpy back roads and scenic byways, the answer became clear: There are more people who believe in goodness and decency and are dedicated to thankless service than there are unconscious scoundrels.

Serendipitously, we found these ordinary heroes—their stories of hope, their tribulations and triumphs—coast to coast. And we found what motivates them—a tie to tradition, a love of family and community, the search for meaning, and heartfelt brotherly love.

Little League and Home Base

Be on the lookout for two bounty hunters, last seen crossing from Ohio into Indiana. One is tall with light hair, blue eyes, and a dimple in his chin. The other is short with dark hair, blue eyes, and she laughs a lot. Armed with tape recorders and cameras, they claim to be capturing "stories on the strength of America."

Here's one.

We left Cleveland, heading west, destination: Perrysburg, Ohio, where my sister Beth and her family live. Right away, we caught our first all-American story—a clue to what makes America tick.

Baseball. In America, there's nothing quite like it. It's where little kids learn how to spit, parents learn how to refrain, and siblings learn to beg for popcorn, hot dogs, and Tangy Taffy.

Only in Little League baseball are foul balls honored as "good tries," balls as "lucky breaks," and hits as just this side of paradise.

My nephew Evan (the only kid I know who hates spaghetti) loves baseball. He's the catcher. Dressed like a knight-in-rubber-armor, he waddles and dives to scoop the rolling prize. He does so with dust in his face and a mean look in his eye, as if to say to his opponent, "Don't try it."

The Cardinals are up to bat. The pitcher throws a fast one. Evan catches it, and the umpire shouts, "STRIKE!" The batter pounds his metal bat on home plate. The catcher beams with joy, searching the crowd for his mom. My sister waves.

"Come on, Brad. You can do it," shouts someone from the stands.

The pitcher winds up and throws another pitch. Then, CRACK. It's a base hit.

"Nice going," shouts a dad. "Nice job" and "Nice hit" are words that follow. It's really a "nice" game.

The runner on first sprints to second. The umpire hollers, "SAFE." Only in baseball do you hear a parent yell, "Way to steal!" Black plastic helmets are pulled on and off as each player takes his turn at the plate. Heads sweating, mouths slurping soda pop, and feet kicking up dust with every move—these kids are cool.

Entering the Ohio Turnpike near Toledo, we headed toward the Indiana border and our campsite, Grand View Bend in Howe, Indiana, on County Road 100 East. So quickly I felt "back home again in Indiana."

I love Indiana for oceans of cornstalks that praise the sun and bow to the wind, for clean white farmhouses that rest on green and golden checkerboard farmland, and for barns, wide with squeaky swinging doors, big enough for John Deere tractors and New Holland balers.

After Bruce engineered the SunnyBrook into slot 10, we unhitched our home-on-wheels and set out for a day of bounty hunting.

Steuben County is known for its 101 lakes. Angola, where I grew up, is the county seat. The lakes are a vital part of summer. As Bruce and I left the trailer this morning, I grabbed my swimming suit. He looked at me in wonder. It's not my normal behavior. But I was back home, and the memories sweet as sweet corn were swirling around me. As a child, whenever we left the house, my mother would say, "Bring your suit along." I think I could water ski before I could swim! I missed this lifestyle when at thirteen I moved with my family to Ohio in 1960. I remember tobogganing at Pokagon State Park in the winter and swimming at Bledsoe's Beach in the summer. I recall ice skating at Henry Park School and wading in the fountain in front of the public library. I loved the May Day procession at St. Andrew's Church and the Angola Hornets Marching Band.

I highly recommend hometown visits. Yes, it's a mixed emotional experience; sad feelings sometimes push aside the joyful memories. But much of who I am today began in Angola, Indiana: values of community, loyalty to friends, and a trusting nature that has served me well. Angola is a place I will always treasure.

Loving Woman Gives Gift of Life

Gifts of the Magi often come through the human heart. Just ask Jana Matal of Sacramento and Vern Heinson of Woodland, California.

Vern and Kathy Heinson were close friends of Jana's parents. Their families owned a cabin in the mountains where they vacationed together.

"Vern has been like a second father to me," Jana said.

On Thanksgiving Day 1992, Jana called Vern, sixty-eight, "to catch up on how he was feeling" after ten months of kidney dialysis. Vern, the once-busy supervisor of a canning company, was very ill. Each day he waited and prayed for an organ donor call.

"When he told me his blood type, O-positive, the same as mine, I instantly thought—I may be a potential live donor," said Jana, who never had such a thought before.

Not chancing it, the thirty-seven-year-old trainer for the California Lottery said nothing to Vern about her enlightened thought until the following September after researching live donorship. "I wanted it to be right with me before I even told him," she said. When she told him, he was reluctant. Expecting this response, Jana asked him to "just think about it."

On Thanksgiving Day 1993, Jana called Vern again. "Well, what do you think?" she asked.

He said, "Yes."

The decision was made, but the process had just begun. Jana had to face others' fears. At first, Kathy said she could not let Jana give such a gift. Jana's mother worried about her daughter's health, and Jana's boyfriend of five years was naturally concerned about her undergoing major surgery. "He told me later that when he heard how strongly I felt about it, he decided to get out of the way and get on board," Jana said.

But there was a spiritual element that made it possible for Jana to set her family at ease. "I just kept saying and believing that everything was going to be fine," she said, touching her heart. "My parents have always been very good to me. My mother is like Auntie Mame, and both of them taught me about loving life and expressing love."

Wasn't she just doing what she was taught?

On February 8, 1994, Jana gave her left kidney to Vern, saving his life and enriching her own forever.

"It was a defining moment in my life," she said. "When I was lying on that cold gurney just before surgery, all I could think was, 'This is really happening.'" Many hours of surgery later, family and friends walked between Jana's and Vern's rooms, checking on both of them.

Three days later, Jana hobbled down two long hallways by herself. What a wonderful moment when the two gowned patients saw each other alive and doing well.

And what now?

Vern is retired and living a full life. He is involved in volunteer work promoting organ donation. Jana, who recalls once wondering what kind of volunteer work she was best suited for, is Vern's partner in public speaking now. They are members of the "Vital Volunteers," a group of grateful recipients and lively donors.

"We are getting the word out about the importance of organ donorship," Jana said. "Fifty-four thousand people are waiting for organs. Eighteen thousand received transplants last year. Of those, fifteen thousand transplants are from brain-dead donors. The rest are from live donors—usually family members."

Then she added, "To qualify for donorship, you have to match for blood type and antigens, which are protein types. There are ninety-two possible antigens, but each person only has six." Vern and Jana matched on two of six.

Organ donor cards are available whenever you renew your driver's license or by calling the Department of Motor Vehicles. "But you must let your family know your wishes about organ donorship because their decision can override your wishes, even if you carry a donor card," Jana warned.

Recently, the Heinsons and the Matals had a four-year celebration of Vern's and Jana's successful kidney transplant and their family's forever friendship. Also, an unexpected honor came to Jana when she was selected to carry the Olympic Torch prior to the 1997 Summer Games in recognition of kidney donation and her volunteer work to promote organ donorship in the Sacramento area.

Uplifting Breakdown

Iowa is the setting of the film *Field of Dreams*. But not all the dreams that come true in the Hawkeye State are fictitious.

From Des Moines, Thomas Thibeault wrote to tell us his incredible story. Enclosed in his letter were two articles published in 1994 in the *Des Moines Register*.

The first is the fun-loving story of Jim Boll, an unusual person who collects odd things. The second is the story of Thibeault and his three children.

Along Iowa's State Route 44 near Dallas Center in central Iowa is an outhouse-turned-City Hall, an old blue Ford Falcon-turned-police-car, and a utility pole festooned with old boots and shoes. Jim Boll, a forty-seven-year-old bachelor, is the founding father of what he calls Boot Hill. To landmark his fictitious town, he constructed the pole that now serves as a drop-off station for worn-out footwear.

"It all started when someone left a boot by the road," Boll reported. "People come from far and wide to add to the collection."

This is just one example of Boll's salvaging spirit. He raises bees, works part-time at his uncle's greenhouse, restores old homes and old cars, and tends his soybean farm. Recently, he went a step further—he rescued a family in need.

Thibeault, age thirty and separated from his children's mother, spent the winter of 1994 converting an old bus into a motor home.

In late spring, after the school year ended, he left New Hampshire with his children, Christinmarie, nine, and twins Shane and Shawn, seven, and headed west toward South Dakota. His destination: a clinic where Shawn could get medical treatment for cystic fibrosis and a place where he could find work and get off welfare. The family had a breakdown along the way—one that changed the course of their lives.

En route, their bus collapsed and was impounded near Urbandale, Iowa. Local social services helped the family find temporary housing at St. Joseph's Shelter in Des Moines. Thibeault's long winter efforts and hopes for a better life seemed to have vanished.

But while in the shelter, the family's luck began to change.

"I was only in town for a day when someone offered me a job," Thibeault said.

Although the job was temporary, Thibeault worked hard. Near the end of the second week, just at the right time, Jim Boll came along. Boll had read about the Thibeault family in the morning paper and called the shelter to see if he could meet with Thomas. At the end of their conversation, Boll said he was going to help, but he didn't know what he was going to do.

The next evening, Boll came back to the shelter, picked up the family, and took them to the Urbandale Police Station where he had arranged for a semi-wrecker to tow the bus. The master of Boot Hill took the whole brood home to his farm.

"It was hard to believe," Thibeault wrote in his letter. "Mr. Boll has done so much for me. I'll never be able to repay him."

Boll found Thibeault a full-time job. He also helped the family by picking up medicine for Shawn and delivering the children to and from child care.

In return, Thibeault helped Boll repair old vehicles, work the farm, and mow the yards. Together they painted the farmhouse.

Although Thibeault is a busy person, raising his children and working full time, he wasn't too busy to report his gratitude. After reading a story in the newspaper about our upbeat news project, he left us a message. "I have a wonderful story to tell about incredible people."

The Thibeaults didn't make it to South Dakota. They found what they needed in Iowa—a home.

Dan the Man

In September 1996, the Sierra Volunteer Fire Department and the Ladies' Fire Auxiliary brought the residents of Sierra County, California, together for a spaghetti dinner. The goal: to benefit the Ramirez family, a family in a life-threatening crisis.

Earlier that summer, Danny Ramirez, age five, complained of a "bad tummyache" to his parents, Ami and Dan Sr. Doctors determined that the child was suffering from a kind of cancer called lymphoma. While Danny was in the hospital receiving chemotherapy, the family received visitors, loads of cards, and many concerned phone calls. All that was very comforting.

"But when the fire department called to tell us they had organized a big fund-raising dinner and that we couldn't turn it down, we were really moved," Ami said with tears in her eyes. "We expected a hundred people, but more than three hundred turned out."

We sat at the kitchen table in the Ramirez home. The faint sound of "rum, rum, rum" was in the background as Danny played with his favorite toy truck in the living room.

While holding Lucas, age two, on her lap, Ami told us how she came to cherish the people in Sierra County. She and Dan had decided to move their growing family to the Sierra Mountains in 1991.

"We wanted a better environment for the boys, a smaller community for all of us," she said.

Dan Sr., holding four-year-old Nicholas on his lap, told how he secured a job with the California Department of Transportation, enabling them to move to the tiny town.

Dan made friends quickly with the men at work. He immediately joined the volunteer fire department, making him a for-sure member of the community.

But Ami didn't make the transition that smoothly. "All of a sudden, the community seemed too small, and I was sort of stuck at home," she said, recalling her loneliness. But soon the community responded. Aware of what young mothers need, someone from the church approached Ami, asking for her help on a project. That's how Ami got what she needed: friends.

Then Dan shifted back to the spaghetti fund-raising dinner. "One of the men who really rallied was Terry LaBlanc, our trash man," Dan said. "He talked for three hours non-stop, calling out raffle tickets for donated prizes. Terry has a bunch of kids."

"The people just didn't want to leave the dinner," said Ami, still amazed at the county-wide response. "People brought food to us for almost a month!"

Then young "Dan the Man," as he likes to be called, jumped up and put his Mickey Mouse hat on his hairless head.

"This is just one of my hats," he announced, tipping the ears on the priceless cap.

Indeed, it is a very special hat. The Make-a-Wish Foundation granted the five-year-old his wish: a trip to

Disneyland for the whole family. All three boys scurried around gathering memorabilia for a show-and-tell session with us.

FAMILY PHOTO

*The Ramirez boys three years later (left to right)
Danny, 8; Lucas, 4 1/2, and Nicholas, 7*

Ami used that moment to give us a progress report. The chemotherapy treatments are completed. Now it's time to rest, regain strength, and avoid germs. Danny's only complaint at this time is about his brother Nicholas.

"He wishes his younger brother didn't want to be right next to him all the time," their mother said.

As for Ami, she couldn't say enough about her appreciation for the community's support, something that was hard for her to accept in the beginning. Dan Sr., who is one of three brothers, just wants to keep his family all together.

The dust was flying when we arrived eighteen months later for a follow-up interview with the Ramirez family. What a joy it was to see Danny, now a lively seven-year-old, with a head of curly brown hair, shirtless and playing dump trucks with his brothers in the yard next to their house.

Recently, Ami stood up in the community church and announced, "The doctors' reports are wonderful. Danny is not only doing well; he's cured. Thank you all for caring about us."

The Heifer Project

How can three "spiritual" cows save lives and end world hunger?

On our way to Cleveland, Arkansas, Bruce noticed a sign: HEIFER PROJECT INTERNATIONAL. "My mom told us about this project," he recalled. "It gives livestock to impoverished families in the United States and abroad."

With that, he made a sharp turn left into the 120-acre ranch. Braced between the dashboard and the rock-solid truck door, I figured this was a detour we shouldn't miss.

BLESSED ARE THE PEACEMAKERS is written across the ranch-style arch that welcomes visitors to the Heifer Project International. The project began as a vision of Dan West, an Indiana farmer and Church of the Brethren minister who was a conscientious objector back in 1938. He envisioned it while feeding a limited supply of powdered milk to starving infants in Europe. When Dan heard the words, "The child could have lived, had we had enough milk," he vowed to find a better way.

"Why not give families a cow, a pig, a goat? Then they can help themselves," Dan concluded.

In 1941, a group of farmers in Middlebury, Indiana, donated three Guernsey calves. They were named Faith, Hope, and Charity. On July 14, 1944, the first shipment of sea-going cows was delivered by "cowboy sailors" to Puerto

Rico. Faith, by then a fine heifer, was given to a family whose ten children had never tasted milk!

Sixty years later, the Heifer Project has provided more than one million families with food and income-producing animals. There is no way to estimate how many lives these animals have saved.

After parking at the Visitors' Center, we were greeted by Lyle Riebe, a newly retired schoolteacher from Minnesota. Lyle, who once taught high school accounting, was teaching the same subject in a new light—sustainable farming. He was to be our tour guide.

"Volunteering these last three months has been one of the most rewarding times of my life," he said as we began the forty-minute driving tour of the farm.

"There are twenty-six volunteers and fourteen staff members, ranging in age from recent high school grads to retirees. The oldest volunteer is seventy-eight," he said.

He explained to us city folk that a heifer is a pregnant cow. "Sending pregnant cows was like sending a double gift."

Then Lyle waved to his friends, volunteers in the organic garden. "At Heifer you learn to build a garden, not just plant it," he said.

On the other side of the road, chickens in tillers were pecking the earth. "It's a way to fertilize the land and raise thirty or more chickens on a small plot of ground," he said.

Then he stopped the vehicle and from the rolled-down window introduced us to a giant pair of gray water buffaloes with brass rings through their nostrils.

"Their names are Briggs and Stratton," he said. "They are valued for the power they provide to small farmers."

On we went. "To your left is the Global Village, four communities designed to teach different levels of subsistence farming. Seventy-five percent of the world makes a living from small farming. And they live in housing like this!" he said.

He described the differences between the Guatemalan hillside farm, the Appalachian house, and the thatched-roof African hut.

"The barrios surrounding cities represent the most impoverished housing—simple shacks made of cardboard and other thrown-away products," he said.

The Arkansas ranch was purchased in 1971 to provide more land to raise a variety of farm animals to be shipped overseas. By 1986 the farm was transformed to an educational center, and the livestock for shipping was then purchased closer to its destination.

A variety of field trips, service-learning projects, and Elderhostel programs here are all dedicated to identifying the causes and possible solutions to world hunger. (Call HPI at 800-422-0474.)

That the United States is estimated to consume thirty percent of the world's resources and that we make up only six percent of the people of the world suggests we need a lesson plan. These statistics, coupled with the complaint of many Americans that they do not experience "making a difference," suggests that HPI serves both the giver and the receiver.

The livestock itself is also a double-good investment. All 101 countries that receive gifts of livestock must adhere to Dan's policy of "Passing on the Gift." Participants agree to give the first healthy female offspring to someone else in need. This is unique to the Heifer Project.

As we stood watching school-aged children make mud bricks from limestone, clay, sand, and water, I remembered the sign arched over the entrance to the ranch: BLESSED ARE THE PEACEMAKERS. How true those words are.

Good Medicine

Good medicine comes in many forms. A sweet dose of music can soothe an aching heart, loosen the pain of arthritis, and put the bounce back into one's step. Paradoxically, a life-threatening experience can be a kind of booster shot. But perhaps the restorative that offers the most vigor per ounce and is guaranteed to regenerate both body and soul is a direct transfusion of grace.

Honky-Tonk Heals

Marion McClure has talent. She plays honky-tonk piano mainly for the residents of nursing homes. She has been playing piano by ear since she was three years old. At seventy, she says, "It's a God-given talent."

A few years ago, Marion moved from Bloomington, Illinois, to Phoenix, Arizona, for health reasons. Her asthma, arthritis, and allergies all got better. But she has a painful case of homesickness.

However, she is pain-free when she plays the piano, a gift that also works wonders for the folks she entertains.

"They just come alive when I play their favorite songs," she said, "and when I'm bouncing around on the piano stool, I haven't a care either."

While playing the piano, Marion encourages the residents to dance.

"It's simple. Whatever you can move, move it," she said. "It's amazing how some who can hardly walk can dance."

One day an elderly gentleman asked Marion to play "Blue Eyes Cryin' in the Rain" by Willie Nelson. He tried to hum it but was unsuccessful. Marion was so sorry, but because she had never heard the song, she couldn't play it.

A few nights later she was up late, "not blowin' the lights out 'til 2:00 or 3:00 A.M.," when she heard the very song on the radio. The next time she went to the nursing home, she made a special announcement and was able to play the song for the gentleman.

"He was tickled," Marion said. "Isn't that what life is all about?"

Man Alive

Why does an unexpected brush with death so often sweep in new life? And why is a near-death experience reported to be exciting for one person, terrifying for another, and "just the way God works," for someone else? We do not have answers, just stories to tell.

Bill Davis, eighty-two, of Pflugerville, Texas, has had two strokes and a triple bypass heart surgery. He's been near-death many times.

"I paid my dues," he said, with a made-up frown. "Why haven't I had an out-of-body experience?"

Bill has spent most of his life as a professional photographer—capturing pictures of life on film. He has an eye for beauty and a curiosity for what illuminates life—the great mystery, of course.

That's why he was disappointed that he didn't see the light at the end of the tunnel when he had his close call. However, when he was released from the hospital, he noticed that something had shifted inside himself.

"Everything looked so green. The earth looked so wonderful. Man alive! I didn't know what I was about to miss," he said. Man—more alive is exactly what he got!

Roni VanSickle from Ft. Lauderdale, Florida, told us that December 4, 1994, is permanently etched in her brain, "like the Kennedy assassination," she said.

Roni and her husband Bob had gone grocery shopping for a holiday party they were planning. Later that night, they were all giggles.

"We were celebrating our fifteenth holiday season together," Roni said. "We got under the covers and cuddled until we fell asleep at about eleven o'clock."

At 2:00 A.M., however, Bob woke with pain in his left side and an icy sweat all over him. "Could my fifty-year-old, physically fit, monumentally strong husband be having a heart attack?" she asked. "Heart attacks happen to our parents, not us."

Feeling that her own heart was going to fly out of her body, Roni pushed all two hundred pounds of Bob into the car and drove like a madwoman through the night to Holy Cross Hospital's emergency department.

"I began to pray," she said. "Because I'm not very religious, I thought I should cover all bases: *'Dear God, I have no picture of a life without Bob. Dear Jesus, have you got one more miracle for us?'"*

When Bob's heart failed to respond to the usual medical emergency treatment, Roni's heart cried louder. "Mary, Mother of Mothers, come here and save him for me."

All of a sudden the miracle came, but not the way she imagined it. The doctor whispered in Roni's ear the name of an experimental drug he wanted to inject under Bob's left arm. It would go directly into his heart. Roni nodded, yes. She had seen something about this on the TV program *20/20*. Within seconds, Bob's color returned and he started talking coherently.

"The miracle is what medical science has learned about saving lives," she said. "God is, indeed, in the details."

Disabled Man Enables Others

"If a disabled person is climbing a mountain, people point and say, 'Look, he's doing that and he's disabled,'" said Martin Duffy, an adventure sports enthusiast and paraplegic. "It's not the disability that's doing anything. It's the ability that's working."

We were sitting at a food court in one of Atlanta's busiest shopping malls, sipping tea and interviewing the world's only disabled hot-air balloon pilot. Duffy, who speaks with a British accent, says his life has been a catalogue of accidents, but it hasn't stopped him.

In 1975 Duffy said he had long hair, platform shoes, and flared trousers. He was working as a junior manager in a posh retail store.

"One night after work and a stop at the pub, I pirouetted backwards out of a second-story window of a Victorian house and landed on my head," he said.

"The ambulance assistants scraped me off the cement. It was a year-long recovery process. Every six weeks I'd wake up and pass out again. Eventually, I realized that I was the lunatic at the end of the hall who kept screaming."

Over time, the screaming stopped and the rehabilitation began. But when Duffy was offered a job in a warehouse, he clearly said, "That's not me."

Since Duffy loves children, he saw an opportunity to help kids in hospitals. He launched an amateur radio show called *Radio Lollipop*. He laughs at advice that radio was too competitive and too stressful for a disabled person.

"Now that's a piece of advice I'm glad I didn't take," he said.

Imagination moved like a slippery roller coaster through the corridors of Queen Mary's Hospital in Surrey, England. Each child had a bedside phone. Between pop records, they called Martin to chat on the radio.

"I'd say something like, 'This is Cynthia Snodgrass, some great chef. She's here to tell us how to make pink bunny pie,'" Duffy said.

The kids would ring in to say they spied the pink rabbit running down their hall.

Later, in another program, Duffy wheeled around the hospital interviewing nurses about the cuts in health care provisions. He stirred social action and built a package of information he took to London radio. They bought it.

"I got into network radio overnight," he said.

The culmination of his media career came when BBC-TV wanted to do a feature on Duffy, the radio reporter in a wheelchair. He said, "No, no, no. Give me a screen test."

That was 1982. Duffy got the job and became a well-known TV anchor and producer. His favorite show was *Scramble: A Call to Action.*

"They would turn me loose in a grocery store, cover it on TV, and everything I could pile in a cart in ten minutes would go to the homeless. The viewers were thinking, 'He's

in a wheelchair. He won't be able to get that much.' Right,"
he said, flexing his biceps.

"What disables me is the spinal cord injury. What handi-
caps me are people's assumptions," he said.

In 1990 a group of athletes approached Duffy complaining that nobody takes wheelchair basketball seriously. Duffy
encouraged them to take themselves more seriously. It paid
off. He produced a tournament series that raised wheelchair basketball to a TV sport in London.

"This is not rehab therapy," Duffy assured us. "It's a
cross between Demolition Derby and ballet."

He knew he'd arrived when a player called to report
that someone in the supermarket recognized him as the
player who had made a dramatic three-point shot.

"That's much better than the usual conversation, 'Can I
reach a can of beans for you?'" Duffy said.

Most touching was the story of how a TV crew once set
up an afternoon of fun for children with disabilities. Duffy
called in the experts—skiing instructors, mountain climb-
ers, horseback riding trainers.

"I told them this was their opportunity to be on TV, to
show off their stuff," he said.

Duffy recalls encouraging a child with spina bifida to
try something new. The child's mother intervened, suggesting her son do something familiar— horseback riding. Duffy
looked the lad in the eye and said, "How about skiing?"

The mother cringed. A week later, she sent Duffy a letter. "Thank you for showing me the ability of my own child,"
she said.

Saved by Amazing Grace

Grace is a heavenly gift with no strings attached. You can't earn it, for grace doesn't depend on what we have done. Rather, by definition, it's what God has done for us. It may be delivered as strength during hard times or the unexpected gift of restored health.

For David Kealey of Pflugerville, Texas, amazing grace saved his life.

David left school in the ninth grade to support his mother and sister. At the time, he thought that was cool. Because he had hot musical talent, good bands sought him. He went on the road, twanging his electric guitar with B. J. Thomas and Johnny Nash and for a while for the Bob Hope show.

Although on the surface he was wildly successful, he felt something was haywire inside.

"There was a hole in me," David said. "Drugs and alcohol seemed to fill it, but something was missing."

David's musical career reached a pinnacle when he landed a job in Houston as the chief recording engineer and general manager of a top-notch recording studio.

"I thought I was God," he said, recalling those days of wine, women, and song.

However, the more success he soaked up, the more booze he drank. The hole inside never filled. "I kept thinking that if I could just get rich enough, it would all fall together," he said.

But it fell apart. The corporation David was working for sold its land to a big developer, and overnight he was unemployed.

"I thought that was the end of the world," he said.

But soon the next get-rich scheme popped up when a friend suggested that they become partners, move to Austin, and buy a bar business.

"Now, this was going to be Mecca," he said with a made-up grin. "But there was just too much beer around, and I drank the profits."

On New Year's Eve 1991, David lay in bed, drunk and depressed.

"I was so low that I pulled my pistol out of the drawer, stuck it up to my head, and was going to squeeze the trigger. Then something at the last second drew my hand away. I shot into my closet and killed about nine of my good shirts. For the first time in my life, I was aware of something greater than myself."

"Amazing," he said. "I lost my will. The god that I thought I was no longer existed."

The next morning, David was admitted to a psychiatric unit. He knew he needed help, but he wasn't ready for much.

"We sat around in group sessions, cutting out paper dolls and talking about, 'What does this grocery bag mean to you?'" he said.

A few days later when he was invited to go to the drug and alcohol unit, he denied that he had a problem. However, to escape the psychiatric ward, he agreed to the transfer.

At first, the 12 Steps were like another language.

"I couldn't make it out," he told us. "They talked about things I'd never known about—alcoholism as a disease, once you are an addict you're always an addict, and there's always a part in the brain that remembers that euphoric feeling. That there is a power greater than myself that could restore me to sanity was the best news."

Characteristically, stories of grace end too good to be true. David completed the thirty-day treatment program. Out of fear of relapse, he continued to go to AA meetings.

As instructed in the program, he prayed and asked for spiritual guidance. His prayers were answered when he was offered a job in Pflugerville where he had heard there was a great AA group. In Pflugerville he met Jeanie, a social worker who would become his wife.

At forty-nine, David finished his GED and took a vocational guidance test. When the test results revealed he had an ability for land surveying, he prayed, "Oh, God, this sounds boring. I can't relate to this. Is it what you want?"

His inner guidance said yes. "It's been the most rewarding profession outside of music I think I could ever have," he told us.

Best of all, the musician hasn't given up his music. On Sunday mornings David and his band deliver rock and roll, biblical style, to the Pflugerville Methodist Church congregation. It's not at all amazing that the people love it.

The Legend of Kate Hill

While camped in Sierra City, California, an old gold-mining town in northern California, Bruce had the opportunity to lead a discussion group on *Gold Rush*, an anthology of stories taken from diaries, books, and letters of real '49ers. The text, edited by Michael Kowalewski, is the centerpiece of the California Council for the Humanities Sesquicentennial Project.

A story written in 1814 by a Methodist minister caught my fancy. The Reverend William Taylor spent seven years teaching on the streets and in the hospitals of San Francisco. In one account he recalls his conversation with a man in a collapsed state who was dying of cholera.

He said to him, "My dear brother, have you made peace with God?"

"No, sir," said the dying man. "I can't say that I have."

"Do you not pray to the Lord sometimes to have mercy on you, to pardon your sins?" Taylor wanted to know.

Though the man had never prayed, he said he did believe in religion. The minister could see the man "was poised on an eddying wave of death's dark tide." Pulling with all his might, "to bring the lifeboat of mercy by the dying man's side," the minister asked if he could pray for him. But, "under the force of the ruling habit of his life," the man coolly said, "I'll think about it," and died.

44

In contrast, I sat on the porch of Sierra City's general store, jotting down the story of how Kate Hill, eighty-six-year old resident, was prayed back to health by three Sierra County ministers—all of whose congregations she attends.

In April 1998, Kate discovered that she was bleeding from the rectum. "As you get older your tissues get thin," she explained. "And I do have a history of diverticulitis."

The active woman, who is frequently seen driving her 4x4 vehicle about town, was rushed by ambulance to Grass Valley, an hour's drive on curvy Highway 49 that winds through the Sierra Mountains. She was losing blood fast.

"I was in intensive care, getting ready to go into surgery when the ministers arrived," she said.

The Reverend Paul Guffin, the Methodist minister of three rural churches, came first. As always, Guffin, who is a gentle man, prayed quietly with reverence. Then came Dr. E. W. Willoughby, the white-haired preacher of The Assembly of God Church. Without hesitation, he took Kate's hand and prayed aloud. Then tall, big-shouldered Reverend Donnie Batcheller arrived from The Lord's Meeting House, a nondenominational group that meets in an old schoolhouse. Batcheller, dressed in a leather vest and cowboy boots, got on his knees and asked for the Almighty's intervention.

Before leaving, Batcheller told Kate that he wanted to anoint her. The beautiful woman, who wears her pure-white hair in a bun like Katherine Hepburn's, said, "Donnie, go for it!"

Kate never did get to surgery. The bleeding stopped.

Heavenly Help

When I was a child, my mother taught me to pray generically; pray for strength. Then if you don't get exactly what you pray for, you will at least have the strength to accept what is. I always thought that was shortsighted. I preferred my interpretation of "Ask and you shall receive"—like placing an order at Sears and driving around to the customer service dock to pick it up.

Several months into our journey, my mom sent a laminated card with an anonymous prayer on it. "Lord, help me to remember that nothing is going to happen to me today that you and I together can't handle."

Wow! The childhood prayer she taught me meant more to me now. Not only did I like the prayer, but also I could appreciate the mystery of life embodied within it.

Single Parent Has Double Duty

"It is an old African saying that the harder the labor, the closer the bond," said Stephanie Wood, hugging her son Malik, age eight. Baseball cap pulled on tight, her big brown eyes wide open, Stephanie, forty-seven, shared her dream come true, about single-parent adoption in our hometown of Cleveland. It was a simple decision about a complex, bumpy process.

As she talked, Malik, also wearing a baseball cap, sat beside his mom, eyes focused and ears perked to the story he loves to hear.

"I read an advertisement in my church bulletin about the need for minority adoptions," said Stephanie, who then lived in Boston, Massachusetts. She decided to make a phone call.

But when the social worker asked the sales executive what her "contingency child care plan" was, Stephanie realized she was not prepared to adopt a child. "So I decided to move back to Cleveland where I would have my family's support," she said.

That winter she contacted a private agency in Cleveland. In April, she moved back to her hometown. In May, Stephanie bought a house in preparation for parenthood. "When I saw the room where he would sleep, already decorated for a little boy, I knew I would have a son," she said.

In line with nature, adoption was a nine-month process. The first few months were the easiest, including the paper work and preparations. "The last trimester was the toughest," she said, rolling her eyes.

The transition from foster care to permanent placement is emotional and time consuming. Stephanie constructed a welcome-home scrapbook for the seventeen-month-old child she was about to adopt. After several get-to-know-each-other visits at the foster home, Stephanie adopted Malik and brought him home to Shaker Heights.

For Stephanie, single parenting was a big decision, tempered by a carefully thought-out process. But no one could predict the twists and turns of corporate life. When Malik was three, Stephanie's business partnership began to fail. She was forced to put her house up for liquidation. She recalls asking a friend, "Why did God give me this wonderful son if I wouldn't be able to provide for him?"

One afternoon, Malik and Stephanie were sitting at the kitchen table as prospective buyers were coming to see the house. When the visitors looked into Malik's room, the room Stephanie had designed two years earlier as the perfect room for her son, she felt a wave of melancholy and surge of sadness.

"I could feel the tears welling up," she said. "So I excused myself to go have a good cry—and I'm not a crier."

Malik sat calmly at the kitchen table and watched his mother leave the room. When she reached the second-floor landing, he called up to her, "Mommy, don't worry, God will help us keep our house."

Some might have brushed off the wisdom of babes, crediting the spontaneous comment as naiveté, but not Stephanie. "I fell on my knees and said, 'Thank you, God, for sending this message.'"

Soon after, Stephanie received two full offers on the house. Both offers fell through. "I was able at that time to make a deal with the mortgage company," she said with a smile. Ultimately, the grateful mother and son managed to keep their home.

Shortly after refinancing the house, Stephanie started her own business, SMART Consulting, offering programs that help people start and develop small businesses. Today she is a successful business owner and a happy mom.

It has not been easy, but it's been worth it.

"The first year I had my son, Malik's godmother sent me a card on Father's Day acknowledging my single parenthood. It said, 'The best present under the sun is a mother and father wrapped up in one.'"

Artist Paints Everyday Angels

Sharon Marie Chester from New Orleans always knew she had artistic talent. She won several art shows in junior and senior high school. But when it was time for college, she turned away from careers considered impractical and pursued social work.

Nearly twenty years later, her husband brought home a newsletter advertising an art contest. He encouraged her to enter. The unpracticed artist accepted the challenge, painting something she already had in mind. "Then I asked God to give me a sign," she said. "Did I really have talent?"

Her picture won Best of Show, the highest honor!

"I knew it was a message, but I still did not pursue art until after Camille died," Sharon Marie said. She began to tell how the death of her daughter changed everything.

"Ever since Matthew, our first child, was very young, he wanted a sister with all his heart," said Sharon Marie. "When he was two, he asked if he could go live in a house where there were other children."

After two years of fertility treatments, Camille was at last conceived. But at twenty-eight weeks, the ultrasound revealed serious congenital problems.

The couple did all they could to save the life of their unborn child. Sharon Marie said that most torturing was knowing that each moment closer to birth would bring their daughter closer to death.

Camille was born on April 29, 1991, with only one ventricle in her heart and minimal lung capacity. Six hours was all the earthly time the Chesters had with their long-awaited daughter. The whole family's heart was broken. Matthew curled up in a corner and cried.

A few months later, Sharon Marie, in a purgatory of grief, had an unusual experience.

"I was alone in the living room when I felt a presence," she said. "There is nothing I can associate it with. It was a clear message, one I heard from all around me. Not in here," she said, pointing to her heart. "It was all around," she explained, gesturing to the entire living room.

Camille seemed to be there, offering her mother love and a gift.

"What this sweet child from the other side could possibly give a common earth mother, I could not comprehend," Sharon Marie said. "So I asked her what she wished to give me. And she answered, 'Anything you want.'"

After four days of pondering, a thought occurred to Sharon Marie: "I always wanted to be an artist, but it seemed too much of a luxury. But if it were a commission, a responsibility, then I could understand its importance."

Camille enabled her mother to reach for the stars. "My assignment is to give Camille's life some meaning through art," said her mother.

She went to her "someday drawer," picking up yesterday's paint brushes and oil paints, and began painting her way through the grieving process. Fifteen pictures later, she completed an exhibit expressing the incomprehensible loss of a child, an exhibit that would help others with similar loss. It was a beginning.

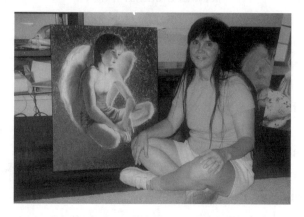

Sharon Marie Chester of New Orleans brings heaven and earth together on canvas.

In 1994 Sharon Marie joined Munholland Methodist Church. As a new member, she offered her artistic talent. At Christmastime, she was asked to decorate the church vestibule with festive banners. The inspired artist went a step beyond.

"The image of two angels flying together simply came to me," she said. "One angel had the face of a man, the other was the angelic face of a little girl."

The finished project, titled "O, Holy Night," went on display during the holiday season in 1995. This is also when Camille's gift went public.

A woman who had lost two family members that year— her grown son to a fatal auto accident and his six-day-old daughter to congenital heart problems—came forward to acknowledge a miracle. The masculine angel had the face of her son. It was obvious he was with his infant daughter.

The grateful woman expressed her joy. "It is the first time I have experienced peace since their tragic loss."

To Sharon Marie, it was affirmation that Camille's short-lived life has meaning and that her artistic talent is worth expression.

Today, from her at-home studio, Sharon Marie paints portraits of children from photos. She calls them "Every-day Angels." The divine touch of including feathery-white wings has become her distinct style. The portrait we admired most was of Matthew, the former only child. Over the years, he has been blessed with a brother and a sister who keep him smiling.

Touched by the Hand of God

In New Orleans we were showered with pennies from heaven when we met Michelle Treen, who introduced us to her best friend, Jill Halpern, a woman who fought for her life against medical science and statistical odds.

Rather than run under a tree, Jill sought the help of her friend and the strength of a hand from above.

Nine years ago, when Jill was pregnant with her first child, she developed symptoms much like Bell's palsy. However, the CAT scan broke down during the test, and the doctors, not wanting to expose Jill to excess radiation, decided she must have Bell's palsy.

"Thank God, the machine broke down; otherwise, they might have terminated the pregnancy in lieu of treatment," Jill said, grateful for retroactive miracles.

Similar symptoms, however, reappeared two years ago with intensity and a more complex outcome. Jill, now mother of two children, was diagnosed to have an inoperable brain tumor.

Jill and her husband, who is a surgeon, searched the medical community for answers. No one gave them a fighting chance. One physician from Tulane University offered a thread of hope.

"Go to New York or Boston," he recommended. "It's too delicate a procedure for anyone in New Orleans."

When her friends asked what they could do, Jill spelled it out: "Go to your church or synagogue and pray." Jill rallied her Jewish friends, while Michelle brought together the Christians.

At Brigham Women's Hospital in Boston, Jill was nearly defeated when she heard for the eleventh time, "We are really sorry, but there is nothing we can do for you."

"I became hysterical," she said.

Her husband's reaction was just the opposite. Emotionally silenced, he was frozen in time, unable to respond.

"I can understand why people commit suicide," Jill said, looking back. "No one gave me hope until Dr. Peter Black appeared in my hospital room."

When Black arrived, Jill was holding a picture of her children in her lap. She recalls, "There was something different about this doctor."

Black simply sat at the exhausted patient's bedside, held her trembling hands, and allowed her to cry.

"I sobbed uncontrollably, pleading for his help," she said.

Finally, this doctor of few words said, "We will operate and remove as much as we can, then radiate the rest out."

His final instructions were to go home, hug those children, and be back at the hospital in a week.

Jill returned home with hope.

The night before Jill returned to Boston, she had an unusual experience. Michelle had given her an audio tape and insisted that Jill listen to it in a relaxed state. It was the soundtrack from the movie *Somewhere in Time*. While floating in a tub of suds and hot water, engulfed in the music,

Jill lost touch with time. Just before drifting off, she remembers praying, "God, I really want to live, but if you want me, that's okay, too."

When she woke up, she recalls feeling touched by the hand of God.

"I knew what to do. I was to tell Dr. Black that the tumor was gone!" she said.

Jill returned to Boston determined to enroll the medical team in a miracle. But on Sunday evening, when Black, the man who had given her hope, entered her room, Jill noticed that something had changed about him.

Fear crept in. Not letting that stop her, she delivered the message: "You are in for a big surprise tomorrow. No tumor!" she announced.

"We will do everything we can," Black said without emotion.

Choosing hope over despair, Jill turned her umbrella upside down, believing that the miracle must be up to her and God.

Monday morning Jill was wheeled into the operating room, family photos and all. Seven hours later, the surgical team, Jill's family, and her friends in New Orleans jumped for joy when they heard the good news. It was not a brain tumor. It was a removable blood clot.

Later, when Black came by to check on his very-much-alive patient, his head was hanging down. He confessed, "You were right all along."

When Jill thanked him for saving her life, he went a step beyond.

"Don't thank me," he said. "It was God."

(Left to right) Michelle Treen and Jill Halpern stand strong together.

Jill looks at these six weeks of terror as a good experience.

"I got to experience God and learned a lot. Tell your children you love them all the time, use your good china, and never think it isn't possible to be touched by the hand of God."

Humbled Surgeon Makes the Cut

With all the controversy that clouds modern medicine, here's a story that reports a silver lining.

David and Michelle Treen were having a difficult time. Michelle was pregnant. A dear friend, Dana, was going to die if she didn't get a lung transplant. And David was heading from their New Orleans home to Texas, where he would take his oral board exams after completing his five-year residency in surgery.

"I went to San Antonio ahead of time to continue preparing as much as I could," he told us. The examiners test applicants for two days. David was to have his turn on the second day.

David knew several other residents who also were locked in their hotel rooms, cramming for the big one. At 5:00 P.M. on the first day, those who had already taken the exam had gathered in the hotel lounge. David sauntered down to get a reading on the test.

"It was miserable," one friend said. He knew he had failed. Another friend felt so-so. Still another said his examiner rifled through a stack of x-rays and came up with an obscure question about an endocrine tumor.

David's morale plummeted. "It's worse than a long shot. It's impossible!" After six months of intense study, what should he tackle in these last twenty-four hours?

He decided to do what he did in college—pick ten possible questions and answer them fully. This would calm his nerves and focus his mind. Believing in the power of what had worked in the past, he would try it again.

As he moped, Michelle called with bad news: Dana's health was failing. Would he please call around the country and locate a lung?

"That's when something inside just shifted, and all my attention went to our friend," David said. "I started praying for Dana and calling around as Michelle had asked."

And about the pressing exam, he said to God, "You have got to carry me on this test. I cannot do it without you."

A calm washed over him, and he drifted off to sleep.

In the morning David was informed he would be testing in the afternoon. Once more he requested guidance from above. "I have a little time to study, what should I study?" he asked.

"Three areas to study just popped into my mind—pediatric trauma, pulmonary embolism, and melanoma," he said.

As if by divine design, the only difficulty David had during the exam was trying to listen to the examiner's question and pray at the same time. One question was about pediatric trauma. Another was about pulmonary embolism.

The crowning glory came in the final stretch. In the last thirty-minute segment, David waited while the examiner thumbed through fifty or sixty photographs. Finally, he picked one and fired the question. It was the x-ray of the obscure endocrine tumor—the same question his friend had.

"I knew I had passed the exam," David said.

When David got back to the hospital, he did what other residents do. To help fellow doctors, he wrote down all the questions and answers he could remember to add to the long list of possible questions that have been asked on the oral exam.

His final advice was a prescription from the heart. "When all else fails, pray harder than you have ever prayed before," he said.

"I knew God was present for me in the exam. And He was also present for others. Dana got a lung transplant and lived three more years. She became our baby daughter's godmother."

An Old Man's Faith

Dave Venable, age ninety-one, from Avon, Indiana, called to tell us about his wife Alice. As a child, she accidentally ate rat poison, causing damage to her heart valve. She was told that she would be dead by thirty-five.

"But I knew from going to church as a teenager that it was possible to be cured by God," Dave said.

After the couple had two children, Dave had to hire someone to help Alice care for them because Alice would get short of breath. He prayed that God would heal his wife. In turn, Dave promised to stop smoking his two packs of cigarettes a day.

"She recovered, and I never smoked another cigarette," he said.

Dave and Alice had three more children.

"When Alice was seventy-five, she went to the doctor for some reason," said Dave. "The girls told the doctor about their mother's history of having heart valve problems. The doctor said he could put a new one in."

But when the surgeon went in to do the operation, he closed her right back up. "He couldn't do it," Dave said. "Alice's heart was in a kind of sack. He said that she had already been healed." Alice lived to be eighty-seven.

"I always thought I ought to give the Lord more than I did," Dave said. "It won't be long before I meet Him, too."

4

Mother Nature Knows Best

T he sanctity of living in community, the innate ability to regenerate from nothing, and the power to move animals and man, not just mountains, belongs to her majesty, Mother Nature. From the depths of the Pacific to the top of Mount St. Helens, she moves with grace and fury, swirling her magic wand. Some humans are so in tune with her call that their lives revolve around her cycles, their souls synchronous with the mind of God.

Walkin' Jim Stoltz

A long time ago, Henry David Thoreau warned, "If a man walk[s] in the woods for love of them half of each day, he is in danger of being regarded as a loafer; but if he spends his whole day as a speculator, shearing off those woods and making earth bald before her time, he is esteemed an industrious and enterprising citizen."

We sat on the end of a bed at the Buckhorn Lodge, in Sierra City, California, talking with Walkin' Jim Stoltz. His skin tanned by sun and wind, the curly-haired hiker sat across from us, his dark eyes conveying his passion for nature and all that is wild.

"I wasn't planning to be a wilderness songster," he said. "I sort of fell into it."

He was dressed in cotton twill shorts, a colorful T-shirt, and well-broken-in walking boots. Leaning against the wall were his backpack, water bottles, and a package wrapped and ready to be mailed home to his wife Leslie in Montana.

Jim sleeps under the stars. This night is his first in three months to sleep in a bed with a roof over his head. He was apologetic. We were in awe.

In 1974 Jim, on a casual walk in Virginia's Shenandoah National Park, met a long-distance hiker walking the Appalachian Trail. After learning that the trail runs from

Georgia to Maine, Jim decided, "That's about the most exciting thing I could do."

That was twenty thousand miles ago. Since then, his energy has been spent raising funds for nonprofit organizations that protect wildlife and preserve the wilderness. We met Jim while he was hiking north along the Pacific Crest Trail that runs approximately 2,700 miles from Mexico to Canada.

He averages twenty miles a day. His boots last about two thousand miles.

"You have to grease them up to keep them from drying out," he said, holding the shoe and tapping the sole. Jim hopes to reach Canada before the new snow flies. That's around October 1.

The tall, lean man has hiked all the trails, the Coast to Coast Trail, the Appalachian Trail, and the Continental Divide through the Rockies. He has walked the plains through North Dakota and Montana and has snowshoed across Wisconsin and Minnesota. Many times he charts his own path using a simple compass. Along the way he writes songs and snaps photos. When not walking, the troubadour plays music and gives slide presentations, sharing his love for all that is wild.

Jim's closest call came while walking the length of Utah in the high mountains. Early one morning, while descending Mount Tipanogos, he encountered a dangerous patch of ice and snow.

"I was coming down off the mountain as carefully as I could and slipped. In a split second, I was sliding down the mountain, trying everything I could to stop," he said.

When Jim realized that he didn't have his ice ax with him and he was headed for the edge, he rolled onto his back. His guitar jabbed into the ice and caught him.

And there he sat near the edge of that cliff for a half-hour, shaking and thinking, 'Thank you, God.'"

He paused. "There is a lot of strength that comes when you know how vulnerable you are, and you honor those boundaries and limits," he said.

The next morning we said our goodbyes to Bruce's parents (whom we'd been staying with), packed the rig, and headed southeast toward Nevada. As we passed through town, we spied Walkin' Jim leaning against a post on the porch of the old country store, and chatting with other hikers. They, too, were packed and ready to roll.

I glanced at Bruce, smiled, and broke into song.

"Get your motor running. Go out on the highway.
Lookin' for adventure, or whatever comes our way."

Yes, we, too, were born to be wild.

As the frontier faded into developed land, America began to consider the wilderness a resource to be enjoyed, not just conquered. Yellowstone, our first national park, was set aside for public use in 1872. The focus, however, was on scenic wonders—geysers, waterfalls, and hot springs—not the wild back country. Not until the 1964 Wilderness Act did we realize the importance of keeping vast amounts of land untouched, unpaved, uncharted by trails, more wild.

Once the West was won, we could grasp what Thoreau was saying: "In wildness is the preservation of the world."

Montana's Walkin' Jim Stolz pauses along the Pacific Crest Trail.

The Orca Earthwatch Project

What attracts people from around the world to the San Juan Islands to study whales? And why do people pay big bucks to volunteer for Earthwatch projects?

Astrid had windblown hair when we met her. She was wearing blue jeans and a faded striped shirt. You'd never guess she teaches computer science as it applies to medicine at Erasmus University in Rotterdam, Netherlands.

Astrid saw her first exhibit about whales in 1986 at the Smithsonian Institution in Washington, D.C. From that introduction, she began an intense study of orcas (killer whales)—how they have the capacity to kill, the intelligence to live peacefully, and the curiosity to reach out to humans, even bonding with them.

"I knew I must see them in the wild," she said.

In 1987 she contacted Ken Balcomb, a zoologist, who had organized The Center for Whale Research off the Washington coast in 1986 to provide baseline data to protect these great mammals.

He opened the project to Earthwatch volunteers in 1987 to help photo-identify and record the behavior of the orcas that roam the deep, cool waters of Puget Sound.

But Balcomb wrote back to Astrid, telling her the project was full that year. He advised her to try again next year.

Astrid is not a woman who gives up easily. She prayed, "If it is meant to be, please let it happen. And if not, please let something equally as moving present itself."

Sixteen days later she received a call saying there was space.

"I think the orcas' mission is to inspire," she said.

For ten days, Earthwatch participants, in groups of five, venture out to sea in trimarans, hoping to sight the orcas. From the quiet boats, pictures are snapped and memories imprinted with the beauty of the black-and-white marine wonders. The mighty orcas communicate through linguistic calls and surface behavior.

"It's a joy to see them leap out of the water in a breach, peck slap, fluke lift, and turn cartwheels in the air," said Stefan, a six-time Earthwatch volunteer from Cologne, Germany, who claims he is addicted to the orcas, the people, and the worthwhile cause.

"Orcas are different from fin whales who travel alone," he said. "They interact and live in community."

From 1967 to 1973, the juvenile population of orcas was dangerously reduced as a result of captures for marine parks. That's why, in 1976, Balcomb founded his center.

He had dozens of stories to share.

"One time we went out to find whales and ran into a thick fog bank. I couldn't see my hand in front of my face. We were about twenty-two miles from home. I had lost track of the whales. Soon they just came porpoising in—fifty of them, very close. For forty-five minutes to an hour, they escorted us through the fog and out. We couldn't find them. They found us!"

Orcas are smaller than humpback whales, bigger than dolphins, and a lot like humans. After studying them for thirty-two years, Balcomb knows their habits.

"They live in pods, like clans," he said, pointing to one of many genealogy charts in the research lab. "They come to maturity in their twenties. Males are introduced to the 'right' females by their mothers. Then they mate. The females reproduce every three to five years until they are nearly forty.

"Then they live thirty to forty years more if they are lucky. The older siblings look after the young calves, and they stay with their mother most of their lives," he said.

In contrast, orcas in captivity live about twenty years.

Two teachers from Los Angeles had their Earthwatch tuition paid by a grant. They are building a science unit about whales, receiving the inspiration they need to inspire students.

"Kids lose out when their teacher isn't excited about science," they concurred, fired up.

A woman from Chicago came to study the orcas because she likes to do group projects that make a difference.

"I don't like cruises. I want to be doing something meaningful," she said, gesturing to her bright yellow cap bearing pins and badges from seven previous Earthwatch projects.

To talk with volunteers who have come so far to be together and to study the whales was inspiring. Best of all I liked what Astrid had said earlier. "Orcas have no home, no nest. Their togetherness is their home." It seemed that everyone at this Earthwatch project felt right at home.

For information about becoming an Earthwatch volunteer, go to earthwatch.org or call 1-800-776-0188.

Digger O'Dell, the Friendly Underdog

The tale of our journey across America would be incomplete without a few heartwarming stories about the pets we have met along the byways—particularly canines.

One of our first ordinary heroes was Simpson, a large black dog with dark eyes that shine in the North Carolina sunlight. Simpson takes care of the Lees, the family he adopted that lives in the great Smoky Mountains.

Each morning this loyal Labrador escorts his family down the winding mountain path, leading the 4x4 truck safely onto the main road. In the afternoon, he listens to the minister who lives at the bottom of the hill practice his sermons from a backporch pulpit. If the sermon is good, he sticks around. If it's rotten, he howls.

In the state of Washington, at a Coast to Coast campsite, Petie, a fuzzy-black toy poodle who dances on his tiny front feet like a fancy circus dog, dazzled us.

But the story of Digger O' Dell, the friendly underdog who cares for the dead in Fresno, California, made us laugh and cry.

I was the quiet passenger, sipping hot coffee and snacking on a warm, sugary cinnamon bun, while Bruce's mom, Billie, drove the car and told tales of how Digger O'Dell came to live with the Madsens and how he became a true son.

"One time when we went camping, an auburn puppy found his way from his campsite, where he was prisoner of a cardboard box, to our campsite, where there were two little boys to play with," Billie said. "He just wanted to be with people."

That was the day Digger claimed the Madsens as his owner, an attitude of being in control that stayed with him all his life.

Bruce's dad, Linc (short for Lincoln), was a mortician. Though the two Madsen sons were well rehearsed in funeral etiquette, the member of the family who followed in his father's footsteps was Digger O'Dell.

In addition to his work with people, Linc owned a pet cemetery—the first of its kind in California. Digger would go there with his master. Digger was the burial assistant. With his head bowed, he would mourn the loss of other dogs while Linc dug their graves, said a few quiet prayers, and piled dirt over their coffins. Digger, a combination of cocker and chow, would stay by Linc's side during each burial.

One day when Linc took Digger to the cemetery and the twosome completed their ritual, something strange happened. When Linc got home, there was no Digger.

"Didn't I take Digger with me?" he asked Billie. Yes, he had, but the chief canine mourner jumped out of the car when his owner stopped at the Texaco to fill up and returned to the cemetery. Linc found the friendly underdog patiently waiting in his favorite spot under the locust tree.

One time Digger was treated to a ride home in the long black limousine. Perched in the back seat peering out of the tinted window, the regal dog sat as if he were ready to say, "Home, James," to his master. When the two arrived on Ferger Street in Fresno, Linc opened the chariot door and the royal canine jumped out.

Digger O'Dell lived to be eight years old. He died of kidney failure. Today he rests in the pet cemetery under the locust tree where he once bowed his head and helped his master bury other dogs. He will be on duty there forever.

Coyote the Trickster

The culture of north central Idaho is stirred by legends of yesterday and traditions of today. The legend of Coyote, the trickster who destroys a great monster giving birth to the Nez Perce Indians in Kamiah, Idaho, keeps yesterday alive. At the same time, the fifty-ninth annual Labor Day barbecue, brings vitality to the town each year.

A long time ago, before the people came and the animals inhabited the land, Coyote learned that a great monster was eating all the animals. He decided to see what he could do. First, he took a bath so he would be tasty to the monster. Then he tricked the monster into eating him. The monster didn't know that Coyote carried with him five stone knives and a fire-making kit.

Inside the monster, Coyote confronts grizzly bear for being so scary. He kicked the bear on the nose. That's why the grizzly bear has a short nose. Next, Coyote confronts a rattlesnake for being vicious, stepping on his head. That's why, to this day, the snake's head is flat. At last, Coyote reached the heart of the monster. There he started a fire and with a stone knife cut out the monster's heart! Then he carved the monster into many pieces, tossing him in all directions and creating the Indian nations. And from the monster's heart, the Nez Perce people sprang up near Kamiah, Idaho. In the Nez Perce National Historic Park (on U.S. Route 12), the monster's heart rests as a huge volcanic mound for everyone to see.

Kamiah, Idaho, population 1,500, is located in the Clearwater River Valley and surrounded by low, rounded volcanic mountains. There we attended the fifty-ninth annual Labor Day parade and free barbecue. Square dancing, crafts, and quilting are favorites in this country town.

"Promenade your ladies down and make a circle, now circle round," directed and sang the caller. Ladies in ruffled skirts and their men in Stetson hats and cowboy boots made this a spectator sport. Bystanders watched with admiration and curiosity, thinking it looks like fun and wondering, "Could I do this?"

Oodles of kids and parents swarmed the city park where the festivities had begun. Sticky cotton candy, crispy corn dogs, and hot vinegared French fries tempted even the most faithful weight watcher. Sometimes it's safer to go the craft route, leaving calories and heartburn behind. Signs to the quilt show, across Main Street, lead us to a major crossing —the crossing of time, for the art of quilting speaks from mother to daughter to granddaughter, a patchwork of family ties.

Alexandria Davis, a native of Idaho, sat at a table among colorful quilted entries. Some were newly stitched, others treasured heirlooms. Quilting since she was fourteen, Alexandria, now in her sixties, still loves the addictive craft.

"My first quilt was made of velvet," she said with a dreamy sigh. "It wore out years ago."

Since then she has completed thirty-five quilts for her children and grandchildren. Behind her hung her most recent brainchild, an award-winning coverlet featuring patchwork photos of the way stations on the road to Elk City, Idaho. But what she really wants to talk about is her 4-H friend, Pamella Cardwell, age fourteen, who won first prize for her Christmas quilt.

"This is a youngster who shears her own sheep, cards her own wool, and sews," boasted Alexandria.

Never before was I interested in quilts. Why today? Is it the quaintness of the town? The friendliness of the people?

We stopped at the Kamiah Kwilt and Kraft store to get a better look at what this quilting addiction is all about. It's easy to become mesmerized by the impressive pictures in Eleanor Burns' book, *Quilt in a Day*. Some patterns are made with reminiscent pastel fabrics, popular in the 1930s. Others are decked out in today's bright, primary colors. All can be worked into a variety of patterns: Dutch Windmills, May Basket, Irish Chain, and Courthouse Steps are a few.

I saw myself choosing colors and fabrics and patterns. I imagined finishing the first project with the next project's pattern already in mnd. Bruce shook my arm, reminding me of our tiny living quarters.

Was it old Coyote and his tricks or the pull of strong traditions that nearly hooked us in Kamiah?

Mount St. Helens Lost Her Top

The Klickitat Indians had two names for Mount St. Helens: Loo-Wit, referring to a lovely maiden who was changed into a beautiful white mountain by Great Spirit, and Tah-one-lat-clah, or "fire mountain."

Mount St. Helens was the most perfect snowy peak in the entire Cascade Range, until May 1980, when she blew her mighty top. Since then, Mother Nature has been busy, rebuilding from the ground up.

The sun is shining, the skies are clearing—it's a perfect day to fly over Mount St. Helens. My cousin, Ken Kadwell, has been flying airplanes since he was fifteen. That's fifty-some years!

"The most dangerous part of flying is driving to the airport," he said. In this case, there's no drive. Ken's Skyhawk 172 is just a short walk from his back door, past the old hay barn and into the minihanger that sits in the corner of his sixty-acre farm in southwest Washington.

"She's dependable, forgiving on landings, and was the most popular plane ever built," he said. "Airplanes have a soul. You have to treat them right."

The seasoned pilot first checked the oil, then the tires. "Just put your hand on the wing, right here," he said to Bruce, demonstrating his technique, "and we'll push her out."

The powder-blue-and-white 1972 Cessna rolled across the cement floor to grassy freedom looking like a friendly Disney character with a silver nose, two windshield eyes, and wing-arms for flight.

We climbed aboard her round-bellied cockpit, Bruce in front, ready for action. I choose the back, time to relax. Ken turns some switches, and the mighty propeller coughs, sputters, then hums.

The Skyhawk taxies to the end of the runway, makes a steady 180-degree turn, and heads down the long gravel path. Ken gives it the go, and we're up and over the tall pines lifting into the Washington skies.

Looking down, we could see tree farms and cattle paths, little winding rivers and glistening creeks.

"That's the Cowlitz River," said Ken, tilting the right wing to bring the shimmering waters into sight.

The Cascades act as a measuring stick for the big beauties that peak above the clouds: Mount Rainier (14,410 feet) on the left, and Mount St. Helens (8,365 feet) ahead in the distance.

"That's Spirit Lake," he said, tilting the left wing down, showing the devastation that remains fifteen years after the eruption. Below are thousands of trees, lying like toothpicks on the ground, some floating in the water.

"The volcano left everything covered with ash. It all died," he said, heading straight for the crater.

An immense hole remains where once there was a perfectly peaked mountain top. After the eruption, Mount St. Helens lost 1,313 feet. "If you look real close, you can see steam still coming out of her," said Ken flying closer. "Look, there are hikers walking on the rim," he added.

The Skyhawk circled the crater's top in a rhythmic pattern, weaving a path through space and time.

While gazing at the jagged crown dusted in glistening snow, the mountain's sides molded with thick brown ash like a smooth glaze on a fired clay pot, you can't help wondering. What was it like to see the whole side of the mountain bulging? Spectators who couldn't stay away and one old man who just wouldn't leave made up most of the fifty-seven who died.

"All the green you see now is new growth," Ken said, breaking the spell as we drew away from the cone. "When she blew out, everything was seared, but now it's coming back," he shouted above the engine. "They tried to harvest the trees, but the ash ruined the saws."

Although the engine was loud, we were quiet—perhaps a response to the beauty of the mountain, today serene. Perhaps a reaction to the devastation below: 232 square miles covered in dismal gray, once rich, green forested land.

A month after the eruption, fireweed blossoms were discovered near Spirit Lake, pushing through the cement-like ash toward the light. Crayfish and salamanders, beaver and frogs somehow managed to survive.

Today, Mount St. Helens National Volcanic Monument is a lovely white mountain, a "fire mountain" that blew her top, and a place to witness nature at its best—destruction and rebirth.

5

Old-Fashioned Love Stories

Who knows when love is about to reach out its tender hand and lift you off your feet? There's a reason for this aerodynamic strategy. Once the feet are off the ground, it's easy to be swept away by love. As time rolls on and love lasts, the feet return to earth, and the work of love begins: to spread that love to others.

Waikiki Beach

We sat at long wooden tables with koa wood bowls before us, maybe two hundred tourists in all. Romance was in the air. After all, there were many honeymooners among us.

Introducing ourselves, we whispered in polite anticipation. Soon the Hawaiian feast began—pit-roasted pork (Lau Lau), poi (taro plant), Lomi Salmon, baked bananas, and fresh-sliced pineapple were starters. Then came what we were all waiting for. The music crescendoed, and the lights lowered.

"Welcome to the Coconut Palm Plantation Luau," sang out the master of ceremonies, a dark-eyed, silky-skinned Hawaiian woman wearing a red-and-white floral dress. "Let's give a warm welcome to the hula dancers," she said.

Then, extending her hand palm up, she invited four handsome Polynesian men and four Polynesian women with long, flowing hair into the spotlight on the dance floor.

Barefoot, a visual feast in colorful native costumes, their collective sixteen hands, eight heads, and eight bodies moved gracefully in unison to the strum of guitars and the lively beat of a drum.

Before there was a written language, the Hawaiians used the hula to record their genealogy and history. Handed down from generation to generation, the hula today is thought to be vital and sacred to the preservation of the Hawaiian culture.

The dances were exciting to watch, but excitement melted into melancholy when I heard my favorite song, "Blue Hawaii." Mesmerized, my mind slipped into the lyrics: *Come with me while the moon is on the sea. The night is young and so are we.*

Dreams do come true in Blue Hawaii, as we learned the next day when we interviewed a couple who met twenty-seven years ago on Waikiki Beach.

Donna, an Oregon widow with six children, was vacationing alone. While walking the beach early one morning, she met a man from Ohio. George was vacationing alone, too. In their late forties, neither had inclination to waste precious time.

"Ours was love at first sight, an opportunity of a lifetime," George said.

"It was the most romantic night," dovetailed Donna. "George proposed that week, under a full moon at a fancy restaurant," she said, smiling across the table at her sweetheart.

But after a few weeks back in Oregon, the blue moon was waning. Donna called George in Ohio.

"I felt I had to give him an opportunity to back out," she said. "At least, he needed to meet my family before making such a big decision."

George thought it was a great idea. When he got off the plane, he presented his bride-to-be with four dozen roses. "I didn't know what she liked, so I brought a dozen each— white, yellow, red, and pink," he said.

A dream came true, they soon married, and Donna and her teenagers moved to Alliance, Ohio. That was just the beginning.

Two years later while vacationing on Nantucket Island, the memory of that blue Pacific moon moved their hearts once more. They decided to make another life-changing decision: to sell it all and start a new life in Hawaii.

After a crash course in hotel management, George gave his employer of thirty-one years a two-week notice. He even forfeited his retirement. The adventurers sailed off, without a job. "Just a firm faith in God and in each other," Donna said.

In a short time, an opportunity to manage a resort hotel surfaced, and George interviewed for the job.

"That Sunday, the church we were attending prayed that George would be hired," Donna said.

An hour later, the hotel owner called with a job offer. Not long after that, Donna was asked to be the YMCA director, doing what she enjoys most—promoting health and working with kids.

During our delightful interview, Donna talked nonstop, and George patiently added his power-packed, two cents worth. We scribbled the story, slurping down juicy slices of Molokai watermelon and sipping hot tea.

At seventy-four and seventy-two, George and Donna Schultz are still working and still in love. Donna volunteers, and George drives the local school bus.

And when the tourist bus, en route to the lighthouse, stops in front of their home, Donna hangs out the Hawaiian flag and welcomes travelers to rest in the shelter of their gazebo. Then she serves them fine tea sweetened with the aloha spirit.

The Great Mud Slide

Caree, a single mother, was living and working in Florida as a sous chef for the Westin Hotels.

"I owned a condo, worked in fancy places, and my son Tobyn was in a private school, but I just wasn't happy," she told us.

Like so many people who suffer from the pain of divorce, Caree no longer trusted love. It was too dangerous. However, as she looks back on those years of independence, she says, "I wasn't ready for love."

Caree decided to move back home to be closer to her family. She bought a ranch in Penn Valley, California, and was raising ostriches and emu when an intuitive girlfriend told her, "Caree, all you need is a little loving."

The advice rolled off her back like water, but the word *loving* stuck. The next day, at the laundromat, Caree ran into Mike, an old friend and former co-worker. He was all fired-up about a job opening at the Red Star Cafe in Alleghany, California. He asked her if she would consider going with him to the quaint gold-mining town, twenty miles off State Highway 49, to check it out. Intrigued, she said she would, but when the day arrived, she tried to back out.

"But I couldn't reach Mike, so I had to keep the commitment," she said.

Sometimes Cupid has a sneaky way of luring humans into the love net.

"I fell in love with the cafe and the town," said Caree. "I decided to stay."

The Red Star Cafe on Main Street has a rough-sawn exterior. The front porch is lined with chairs facing the Sierra Mountains. Inside, the coffee is always brewing. Open from early morning until after dinner, it's the gathering place for the locals—gold miners and their families.

Simplicity is woven into the old lace curtains, history pounded into the wood-planked floors, and laughter printed on the colorful tablecloths. On the wall glows the 1993 picture of the miners, dirty overalls, smiling faces, arms wrapped around one another's shoulders, celebrating a million-dollar day. These guys are happy.

Caree saw Mark, a miner, in the restaurant picture and thought, *What a hunk. He has to be married.* That hunch was solidified when Mark's three children showed up at the cafe on a regular basis.

Meanwhile, Mark showed similar unspoken interest. Every day for about two weeks, the underground foreman at the Sixteen to One gold mine ate breakfast, lunch, and dinner at the Red Star Cafe.

"But we never said anything to each other," Caree said.

It turns out he was single. Someone told Mark that Caree was single, too.

Maybe it was the mouth-watering burgers or the piled-high ham on rye that sealed their fate. More likely, it was Teresa, Mark's eight-year-old daughter, who jump-started the relationship. One day, in front of Mark, she asked Caree, "Do you want to be his girlfriend?"

Then Teresa turned to her dad and said, "Do you want to be her boyfriend?"

"After that, we became inseparable," said Caree. She and Tobyn moved in with Mark and his brood.

Though love captured their hearts, there was no talk of marriage, no need to rush into a scary commitment, until the night of January 1, 1997, a mere four months after they met.

Rain had been dumping all day long. In the middle of the night, Caree heard glass breaking and woke Mark. They looked out the window and couldn't make out what they were seeing. Could they be looking at a missing hillside? Then waves came whooshing across the road.

"It was the water line breaking," she said. A huge mud slide was beginning.

The couple, afraid that the mountainside house was about to slide off, woke the children: Tobyn, thirteen, Teresa, nine, Wade, eight, and Steven, seven.

"We all ran from the house. The kids were all crying and clutching their blankets and pillows," Caree said.

When the children were all tucked into a neighbor's extra beds, the homeless adults sought refuge nearby in the gold mining office. There, on the night of the great mudslide, Mark Loving asked Caree to be his lawfully wedded wife. She said, "Yes."

For those who may have given up on love, we suggest letting fate play Cupid.

Hal the Flying News Man and Sweetie Pie

Birds on a wire sit serenely watching the sun setting on the Sierra Valley, elevation 5,000 feet. For miles, golden fields sweep across cattle-grazing land, echoing memories of gold mining days and the adventurous '49ers.

One hundred years later Allene and Hal Wright unearthed a different kind of gold, the *Sierra Booster*, "a pictorial newspaper aggressively devoted to the best interests of Sierra, Eastern Plumas, and parts of Lassen, Nevada, and Yuba counties."

Hal explained, "I was working for Rockwell [International] as general foreman of a plant in Oakland, California, when I got word to get ready to move to Nebraska."

Instead, the Wrights flew the coop, heading north to the Sierra Mountains.

"I wanted to start a newspaper. I thought it might be a good thing," said the tall, lean man wearing blue jeans and a white turtleneck shirt.

White hair neatly combed and blue eyes focused, Hal told the story. In the 1930s he was a gold miner. That's how he discovered the beauty of the Sierra Valley. After a mining injury, he worked for a while in Nevada City for a newspaper where he learned the trade. The news was in his blood. His grandparents, Horace and Christie Wright, started the first newspaper in Pasa Robles, California.

And that wasn't all that was in his blood. Hal's ancestry dates back to the Wright brothers and Kitty Hawk, making the editor and publisher of the *Sierra Booster* the ideal person to deliver the news by airplane as a kind of Pony Express of the sky.

"But newspaper work is a losing proposition," said Hal, who learned to fly when he was forty-nine. "I do it for fun. I don't know any other newsman nutty enough to deliver papers by air!" said the man who flies a 600-square-mile paper route in his 1948 Aeronca twin-seater.

Hal is still soaring above the clouds at age ninety-two, but keeping up with today's technical demands isn't always a breeze. Recently, the Federal Aviation Administration tried to dismount the longtime pilot.

"They decided I was too old to fly," he said with a made-up frown. "I didn't think that was right, so I challenged them."

Hal was required to undergo a thorough physical exam.

"I had to get three doctors to go through this thing," he said. "And I passed it all right."

Then he smiled and added, "Don't forget I'm one of the few survivors of the 1906 earthquake."

He is also the oldest alumnus from the University of San Francisco, class of 1927.

However, more than age and wisdom is needed to produce and deliver a successful newspaper, one with a circulation of 3,500 and subscribers in every state.

Operating the newspaper is a family affair. The Wright's daughter, Jan Buck, interviews, enters data in the computer, writes stories, and cuts and pastes together the twice-monthly newspaper. Then she flies with her dad, delivering the product from above, while her mom, Allene, writes, manages, and assists from the ground.

"So much of what's in print today isn't newsworthy," said Allene. What the *Sierra Booster* boosts is community spirit, mostly upbeat news, something Hal says is easy to find.

"I don't think you can get more than one percent of the news," he said. "I just talk to people. There's always something to write about." Then he paused, entering into a deeper conversation.

"I have to tell you about Allene," he said, reaching for a pink box on the coffee table. Opening the treasure, he disclosed a lock of auburn hair. As his hand touched the precious past, Hal spoke lovingly of the woman he calls, "Sweetie Pie," his bride of fifty-six years. It was truly a picture-perfect moment.

Then, breaking the spell, he asked, "Oh, did I tell you I'm a UFO?" The United Flying Octogenarians is an organization with more than 150 members in the U.S. "And the membership is growing," he said, gesturing one hand in the air like a skyrocket.

Hal and "Sweetie Pie" moved to the Sierra Mountains to launch the *Sierra Booster* and struck a new kind of gold, the uplifting airborne news.

They told how they moved to Loyalton as a young couple with lots of hopes and dreams, how they raised their family in Sierra Valley, and how they still work together to spread positive news throughout Sierra County.

The Caldwell Couple

When we were on our way back to Cleveland from Texas to visit family and friends, we took a wrong turn that landed us in the right place at the right time.

"How did we get here?" Bruce asked when we passed the Caldwell, Kansas, city limits sign. To our left, a band of breathless teens was pedaling bikes. Along the river bank, another group scurried out of canoes as a handful of kids on horseback trotted by. The scene looked like a relay.

We parked on Main Street and followed the sound of a foot-stomping country band playing "Oh, Them Golden Slippers." The teens we saw down the road, participants in the annual Ghost Rider Trail Race, were just crossing the finish line. The crowd, many dressed in cowpoke attire, cheered.

We were thrilled to find ourselves at the 130th anniversary of the Chisholm Trail, the longhorn cattle trail that the McCoy brothers blazed from south Texas to Abilene, Kansas, in 1867.

According to the historic marker, Caldwell, an old cow town, was a home to gunslingers, cowboys, prostitutes, Indians, saloon keepers, and criminals. A Wichita editor wrote, "As we go to press, hell is again in session in Caldwell."

Today, however, the badness has faded like old gunsmoke

from a Colt .45. What remains is a proud, quiet farming community.

At the Hitchin' Post restaurant, we met Russell and Charlotte Sawyer. Between bites of "honey-stung" chicken and country whipped potatoes, we enjoyed the story of how, in the 1920s, Russell's granddaddy drove his new model-T Ford right through the end of the barn.

The couple suggested that we visit the civic center where local artists had their work on display. Russell had some woodcarving to show us.

When we arrived, Russell, whom we learned had been carving wood since 1938, was sitting on a stool, balancing a square piece of wood between his thighs. Using a wooden-handled tool, he began working the wood.

Then I realized that this man, who walked more than six feet tall and held his body like a proud cowboy, had only one arm.

Admiring the finely carved lines of a moose taking shape from a hunk of white pine, I asked, "How do you do that?"

"I just never thought I couldn't," he said.

Russell lost his arm when he was thirteen. After a nasty compound fracture, he developed gangrene. His left arm had to be amputated to save his life.

"Nobody would hire a one-armed man, so I started my own welding shop. Then I had a construction business and studied electronics," he said.

Everything Russell did was self-taught and by hand. He reached inside his pocket, and even before pulling out the pocketknife, he opened the blade to demonstrate how well he manages.

There was something warm and wonderful about Russell and Charlotte, who had raised four children in Caldwell.

"One time I noticed that our five-year-old son Randy was being too quiet," Charlotte said. When the curious mother peeked around the kitchen door, she saw the child sitting on the living room floor, patiently trying to tie his shoe with one hand. Today, he's an artist and coach at Caldwell High School.

Russell became a great roller skater. "When I started skating, I couldn't even stand up on the silly things," Russell said.

At the end of his first outing, the owner of the rink asked Russell if he knew how many times he had fallen that day.

"I wasn't counting," said Russell.

"Forty times," said the man. "But if you're that determined to skate, it will never cost you a dime to skate here again."

Over time, Russell became quite skilled. He was so good that he became a skating instructor, teaching hundreds of people how to skate. That's how he met Charlotte.

"I tried to teach her how to skate. It is the only failure I ever had," he said with a big smile aimed toward his wife of fifty-five years.

"I figured if she couldn't skate she might need help with other things, so I married her on Valentine's Day."

Skipped Ship for Love

As a teenager, when Mena heard Mario Ronghi singing, her fate was sealed. "I told my cousin I was going to marry that guy," Mena said.

But it wasn't that simple. When she was eighteen, her parents moved the family from Italy to Springfield, Massachusetts. Oldest of five children and the only daughter, Mena was torn. How could she honor her parents and leave her sweetheart behind?

We sat at the Ronghi's kitchen table, sipping coffee, slurping rum-filled chocolate candy and munching on thin slices of Italian *pan forte* (cake). Mario gestured with his hands, telling the story of how he met Mena and how he became an illegal immigrant for love forty-two years ago. Like wildly eating popcorn at an action-packed movie, we listened, engrossed, consuming the entire plate of Italian goodies as the story progressed.

They met in July 1954. They fell in love. Then something unexpected happened. Mena's relatives from Springfield, Massachusetts, came to visit. "When they saw how we lived, tightly packed like sardines, they said, 'Your mother is a U.S. citizen. Why don't you come to America?'"

"My mother came to America for us," Mena said. "I had to come." But as soon as they were settled, both her parents became ill.

Back in Italy, Mario got a job on a ship and sailed for America to find her. From the New York harbor, the lovesick man hailed a taxi. Then, not speaking any English, he waved his hands and puffed, "choo-choo, toot-toot," and the cabby delivered him to Grand Central Station. At the station, Mario's eyes widened. There were many Springfields and hundreds of trains.

"I pointed to some gold letters, bought a ticket for $5.50, boarded a train, and prayed it would take me to Mena's Springfield," he said.

"I was dressed in a double-breasted suit, and I looked like a gangster, but all I could think of was finding someone who spoke Italian. I had no money, no passport, and no papers," he added.

Eventually, the train arrived in Springfield, Massachusetts. Mario grabbed another cab and was soon on the street where Mena lived. But when he knocked on the door, Mena refused to answer. There had been a murder in the neighborhood, and the people dared not open their doors to strangers.

Finally, her mother opened the door, and Mena began to shout, "How did you get here?"

"I don't know. I was in a trance," Mario said, recreating that memorable moment in October.

It was like a fairy tale come true—until Mario remembered that he was on a two-day pass from his ship.

"Without a blood test, we couldn't get married, and that would take days," he said. "Mena needed me. Her parents were ill. So I jumped ship."

Mena told people that Mario was on a three-month visa.

The couple was married in December, but that wasn't the end of the story. "By immigration law, even if you marry an American citizen, you are still illegal," Mario said.

And becoming legal was last on the list of ever-growing problems. Mena's mother died, leaving hospital bills, funeral expenses, and the rising cost of feeding four brothers ages eight, ten, fourteen, and sixteen. Three months after the young couple paid off the mother's bills, Mena's father died.

"Then I became pregnant," Mena said.

For five years, Mario was a hard-working, illegal immigrant. He learned a trade, supported his growing extended family, and taught himself English.

One day the pressure of being a fugitive caught up to him. He turned himself in, confessed his guilt, and explained why he stayed in America. "But he always paid his taxes," Mena chimed in.

"They could have deported me, but they decided to drop the charges," said Mario. Three years later, he became a U.S. citizen.

Finally, it was Mena's turn to share their happy ending.

"Mario put all five of our children through college," she said. "He used to come home around 6:00 P.M., kiss the kids so that they knew they had a father, and go back to work. He worked in the space program and became an inventor. He always thinks, 'How can I make things better?'"

And make things better is just what Mario did. Mena's mother had come to America so that her family could have a better life. Because of Mario, the sweetheart who couldn't stand being left behind, they did.

6

Keep the Home Fires Burning

Love fuels the fire of devotion that unifies families and fosters the spirit of community. Love is inclusive and expansive. It takes many forms. Open arms, open minds, open hearts, and open invitations are but a few.

For Love is patient. Love is kind. Love protects, always trusts, always hopes, always perseveres. Love never fails. (1 Corinthians 13: 4, 7, 8)

Three Is Not a Crowd

If the Hallmark Hall of Fame is hunting for new holiday scripts, the touching story of Carol and Ed Lillibridge of Cupertino, California, might be of interest.

In 1985 Carol, forty, and Ed, thirty-eight, had been married for ten years. They had no children—just two active careers and the fear that they were becoming yuppies. Because they always wanted kids and couldn't have them, they decided to adopt.

"At our age it would not be a simple process," said Ed, a Stanford grad who works with computer software. "It would have to be a private adoption."

Carol, the executive director of an agency that helps people face life-threatening illnesses, was determined to find a child. "I found a direct mailing expert and told him the zip codes we were trying to reach in states that were more amenable to private adoption," she said.

When the list was complete, the couple gathered a group of friends together for a stuffing party, sending out 5,000 letters and pictures to physicians who might know of someone needing a home for a child.

Thirteen days later, a young woman called. Ready for action, Carol and Ed flew to Las Vegas to meet the mother-to-be. She wasn't due for several months, but here was a beginning.

A few weeks later Carol received another call—this one from a friend whose distant cousin was interested in placing her newborn son for adoption. "When we called, the new mother was very anxious on the phone," said Ed. "There was an urgency in her voice. She said if we were interested, we must come right away."

The couple dashed into action. They called the airlines, made arrangements, and flew to Arizona that very day, arriving just after midnight, November 11.

"The mother met us at the front door with the baby, clothes and all," Ed said. Instantly, he became a father.

Leaving with baby Tim bundled in their arms, Carol and Ed stopped at an all-night cafe to catch their breath and gather their thoughts. In the middle of the night, far from home, the couple felt overwhelmed at being new parents. "The waitress was so helpful," Ed said. "She sterilized Tim's bottle and comforted us."

From the cafe, Carol and Ed telephoned their attorney back home. "He said just to get home and we would work out the legalities from there," said Ed, recalling his flood of immense relief.

They didn't know it then, but this precious infant was just the beginning.

Five months later, Carol and Ed received another call— this time from the first mother-to-be in Las Vegas. "She said if we wanted to be there for the birth, we should leave now!" said Ed, repeating the instructions.

Once again the couple grabbed airplane tickets and prepared to fly off for a second chance at parenthood. But this time the hand of fate grabbed back.

Just minutes before they left, Ed's sister in Southern California called to say Ed's niece had been in a fatal auto accident and that his great-nephew, Jeff, age six, had been orphaned. Could they help?

"Of course," Ed told her. "Right after we swing by Las Vegas and pick up baby Tom."

Thus the Lillibridge family was born. In five short months, Carol and Ed became the parents of two infants and a first grader, all boys.

"Jeff slept under the piano. Tim had a regular crib. Tom was in a portacrib, and my mother, who came to help, slept on the couch. We all lived together under one roof," said Carol, still amazed.

"I was riding the wave—one hundred percent out of control, and in God's hands," she said. "I had to reassure my staff at work that I wasn't leaving them and convince my mother that I wasn't crazy."

Then the real heroes arrived. A real estate friend found them a bigger house. Ed's father found them a family van, and gifts began landing on their front porch.

"People were giving us loads of baby stuff," said Ed.

But the Lillibridge family was not yet complete.

Now they needed a full-time, live-in housekeeper so that Carol could continue in her vital role at the agency. After a brief newspaper search, they found her—a woman who was caring, calm, and experienced with children. One of her greatest assets was her six-year-old granddaughter who became an instant companion for Jeff.

And that's how a career-minded house became transformed to a lively, child-centered home.

"That first Christmas when we were all together, I felt so fulfilled," Carol said. "It was one of the happiest days of my life."

Wired by Faith

Why do bad things happen to good people? And why do some people survive in spite of horrendous odds?

Patricia Sweeny, a widow in her sixties from Indianapolis, saw her doctor because of bleeding from one of her breasts. The doctor didn't seem concerned, but she was inspired to make an appointment at the Mayo Clinic in Rochester, Minnesota, for another opinion.

Not wanting to alarm her five sons, Patricia made flight reservations and told only her eldest son who lives in Minneapolis. Within a few hours after the examination, the Mayo doctors sent Patricia to nearby St. Mary's Hospital for the removal of some cancerous cells. She had to go back to surgery the following day because the doctors were concerned that they had missed some cells. And though the prognosis was good, as a precaution, Patricia was asked to come back to the Mayo Clinic in a month for radiation therapy.

On the day of her fourth radiation treatment, she experienced terrible pains in her head, collapsed, and was rushed to the emergency department. The lively woman had suffered a massive stroke. She stopped breathing twice.

Her prognosis didn't look good. Luckily, a friend who had come to Rochester to be with Patricia became her lifeline, calling her son who lives in Minnesota.

"The doctors needed to know what to do," said Patricia. "My son, who knows I'm a fighter, said to do everything they could to save me."

Then she paused to express gratitude for Divine Providence. "If you are going to have a massive stroke, the place to be is the Mayo Clinic. Doctors from all over the world come there to learn about working with stroke patients."

Patricia remained in a coma in the intensive care unit. Every seventy-two hours, the doctors would decide to wait another seventy-two hours. They feared she would have another stroke. Her heart and lungs were wired to high-tech monitors. Above her bed, the continuous IV drip, drip, dripped droplets of hope. By now all five sons were by her bedside, praying.

"It must have been horrendous for my family to watch me struggle," she said. "But I never suffered. I was totally out of it. The doctors drilled three holes in my skull to draw the blood off my brain. Some of the doctors wanted to put a shunt in my head. Others said there was no use."

After six-and-a-half weeks, Patricia's sons brought their mother back to Indianapolis in a Lear jet, determined to keep her alive. She was still in a coma, not expected to live.

A few months later, at the nursing home, her sons remembered about the shunt and asked the Indianapolis doctors to consider it. Why not try it?

On a Friday afternoon, Patricia was sent for her umpteenth brain scan, and on Monday morning the shunt was surgically inserted.

"A week later, I woke up. I was alert and in the world again, but I didn't know what happened," she told us. "Each day my sons told me a little more of the story."

Then the work began. Patricia, who had not walked in months, was belted into a wheelchair and rolled to physical therapy.

"I had to learn to walk and talk again," she said, recalling six weeks of physical therapy. Like the crutches and braces cast off at Lourdes and Fatima, her wheelchair, walker, and cane remained behind. When she returned home, she required minimal care.

"My doctor says my recovery is a miracle," she said.

When Patricia was close to death, she never saw a light at the end of a tunnel. She wasn't visited by angels or given inner messages about the meaning of life. However, she loves to tell her story of hope and says "never to pull the plug."

"My sons never stopped praying, and they never gave up believing that God was helping us. They just knew their mother would make it."

Teenager Is Cool Kid

It takes a whole family to shepherd the flock. It also takes a little intervention, a lot of love, and a fair share of risk—when it comes to teenagers on the run.

"My brother Greg has three children from his first marriage to Ann," wrote my friend Sue Ellen from Cleveland Heights. "After the divorce, Ann was determined to raise the children by her own rules. She believed that children should never hear the word *no*."

"As you can imagine, the kids grew up without boundaries, and all hell broke loose when they became teenagers," Sue Ellen said.

One summer day, Ann was at her wit's end. She deposited the children on Greg's front lawn—no warning, no discussion, and no instructions. Quickly, an avalanche of miscommunications tumbled between fourteen-year-old Steven, the eldest, and his new stepmother.

"They squared off like prize fighters on a regular basis," said Sue Ellen. "On the other hand, my brother used the problem-solving skills learned at our mother's knee—sullenness and blame."

Neither approach worked, and Steven, who had tested his limits to the max, felt quite lost and ran away from home, making his way from Berea to Coventry Road. There, he lived like a fugitive on the streets for two months with warrants out for his arrest from the Parma and Cleveland Heights Police Departments.

One summer evening, Sue Ellen, on her way to the Centrum movie theater, spied her nephew in front of the Arabica Coffee House.

"I never got to the movie. I just couldn't go in. When I saw Steven, I hugged him and started crying," she said. "I think that surprised him. We talked."

"Luckily, Coventry is my turf," said Sue Ellen. "I alerted some friends to the situation, asking them to call me when they saw my nephew."

Not long after that, the concerned aunt got the call. Again, Steven was outside of Arabica with a group of friends.

"I headed straight to the corner of Euclid Heights Boulevard and Coventry Road," said Sue Ellen. "I didn't know what I would say. I just knew I had to talk to him again."

When she arrived, Steven was surrounded by a group of teens that obviously cared about him and were protecting him. He was wearing tattered clothes and had safety pins inserted through various body parts.

"He looked oddly young and terribly vulnerable," Sue Ellen said. "I walked up to him and touched his arm."

Though her nephew looked frightened and about to run, Sue Ellen maintained a gentle, yet firm hold on his arm. With tears in her eyes, she assured him that she only wanted to talk. "I told him that I wasn't going to turn him in. That was his decision. I just wanted to know he was okay, that he was safe," she said.

There were more meetings.

"We talked about lots of things: What were his plans? Did he want to go back to school? Which school? Where did he want to live? How did he want to live?"

As summer waned, Steven began to realize that he had to go back home, but which home? Moving back with his mother didn't seem to be the direction he was going. He could, however, see himself returning to his father's house. But to do that, he would have to make peace.

"In a move that really made me proud, he apologized to his dad and stepmother. He asked to be allowed to return to his family," said Sue Ellen.

Recently, Steven celebrated his sixteenth birthday. He is off probation and back in school at Berea High. A few times he has visited his aunt for the weekend. Sue Ellen admits that when Steven visits, she doesn't see much of him because he is busy hanging out with his Coventry friends. But that's okay.

"I just enjoy having this really cool kid in my life," she said.

Conspiracy for Love

On our way from Cleveland to Coldwater, Michigan, to visit my Aunt Zoa and Uncle Lewie, I boasted that if we were lucky, Zoa would pan-fry a pile of Lewie's famous blue gills for us.

Though he is nearly ninety, Lewie is still an avid fisherman. We arrived at lunchtime, and sure enough, Zoa was standing at the kitchen counter, dusting flour and cornmeal over egg-dipped fish.

We sat at the kitchen table, telling family stories. Lewie told how he met Zoa in the sixth grade. For Easter that year, he took her a real chocolate egg. But when he got to her front door, he panicked and asked my dad to give it to her.

When Zoa asked about our children and grandchildren, we rattled off the latest good news. As my aunt gently placed several pieces of fish into a shallow lake of sizzling oil, she shared a note of sadness.

"Sometimes I feel we have been cheated out of being grandparents," she said. "We don't get to see our grandchildren or our kids very often because they live so far away."

I leaned up in my chair. In all these years, I was not aware that my favorite aunt and uncle were lonely for their children. Before I could find a word of comfort, Zoa shifted her tone.

"But you know, we are blessed. We have been adopted by some of the youth at our church whose grandparents live out of town. I guess it all works out," she said.

After lunch we slid into comfortable living room chairs to reminisce. We watched a video of my cousin Lynn singing with his barbershop quartet. We listened to fun stories about Ken who rebuilt one of Liberace's pianos. We heard about Dan's plan to move to Idaho and saw pictures of Brian's daughter.

The little girl inside me who loves to hear stories asked my aunt and uncle if they would tell my favorite one, the story about their sixtieth wedding anniversary. Aunt Zoa's entire face lit up. I could even see her eyes glowing behind the dark glasses she has worn all these years due to a childhood injury.

"Now that's a great story," Uncle Lewie said.

It was the day before their sixtieth wedding anniversary. Neither Zoa nor Lewie was thinking too much about it since they had a gala event for their fiftieth anniversary. Late in the evening, they were resting in the living room of their ranch-style home when there was a knock on the back door.

A surprise visitor, their youngest son, Brian, who lives in Holland, Michigan, said he was in town on business and stopped by to show them his new camcorder.

"We did a lot of visiting, and Brian played the organ," said Zoa. "He stayed longer than we thought he would, but we were so happy to see him that we didn't realize how late it was."

At 11:45 P.M. the front door bell rang. "Now who could that be?" asked Zoa.

Lewie went to the door and there, all smiles, stood their oldest son, Ken, who lives in Onalaska, Washington. "Well, I thought I'd come and help you celebrate your anniversary, Mom and Dad," he said.

After lots of hugs, Ken said, "Let me go to the car and get my luggage." When he returned, he was arm in arm with his brother, Lynn, who had arrived from Canby, Washington. Meanwhile, Brian recorded the family fun on his new video camera.

After more hugs, Lynn excused himself to get his luggage and promptly returned with brother Dan, who had come from Aloha, Oregon.

The family was all together for the first time in eight years!

It wasn't easy to coordinate so many flights, but the lasting memories were well worth it.

Just Ask Smiling Arnold

This year in New Orleans, bakers shoveled from their ovens an estimated quarter of a million King cakes—braided, circular coffee cakes sprinkled with sugar in the traditional Mardi Gras colors: purple for justice, green for faith, and gold for power.

Baked right into the sweet dough is a prize: a plastic baby. The cry, "I got the baby!" determines the king or queen of the ball. The one who finds the hidden trinket is also expected to hold the next ball, and the season goes rolling on.

The tradition of celebrating the feast of the three Magi with this special cake begins the twelfth day after Christmas and dances on until Mardi Gras, which is generally mid-February.

We learned about King cakes and other Louisiana traditions west of New Orleans in Paradis, Louisiana, where we met Jean Boyer and her seventy-nine-year-old friend, Arnold Hymel. Jean, thirty-six, is a self-appointed cheerleader for the elderly. Why? Because she values tradition and those who keep it alive. Three years ago while writing her "Silver Streak" column for the St. Charles *Herald-Guide*, she interviewed Mr. Hymel. In February she invited us to her home so that we could meet him.

"Mr. Hymel is one mighty strong volunteer who gives from his heart," she told us. Then, using the blunt end of her writing pen, she touched the gentle man lightly on his chest like a queen placing the flat edge of a sword to declare a knight. She added, "He's also big on spiritual strength."

Arnold's greatest strength, indeed, is helping and encouraging others. He got sixty seniors to join the Norco Senior Activity Center by making personal phone calls to invite each one.

"But it's more than doing good," said Jean. "It's about producing goodness in the world. Mr. Hymel stands by his family, which for him includes not only his children and grandchildren, all living within five blocks of him, but also the whole community. Family 'closeness' is behind everything he does, whether delivering the elderly to doctor appointments or delivering meals to shut-ins."

As we spoke, Jean was cooking up a roux. The aroma of fall-off-the-bone chicken and savory sausage filled the kitchen. She sliced the French bread and scooped out creamy potato salad loaded with eggs and pickles. We sat around the kitchen table sharing stories, filling our bellies, and warming our hearts over the fire of Louisiana hospitality. It's tradition.

Arnold spoke of his father, who was the overseer of a sugar cane plantation nearly one hundred years ago when sugar was king and the railroad was a newfangled operation. He shared stories about his mother and how he admired her for keeping the family together after his father died, leaving her with six young children.

Arnold's only regret today is that when his French-speaking mother died, so did his French. But you wouldn't know it. His accent is thick as molasses, and his friends call him *Parain*, which is French for *godfather*. Others call him Smiling Arnold.

Jean is smiling, too. From a back bedroom, she lugged a heavy genealogy album and plopped it on the kitchen table. We flipped through pictures of her family growing up in the rich cultural diversity of New Orleans, a history grounded in America since 1724.

For dessert we delighted in King cake. "It's all the craze," Jean said, carefully carrying the bakers' cardboard with both hands.

How perfect that Arnold got the prize in his first bite. "In all my years, I've never been the one to get the baby!" he said, smiling.

After lunch, we all piled into Jean's car and zipped past sleepy bayous, busy fishing docks, and lonely above-ground cemeteries to the Destrehan Plantation, built in 1787. There we learned that when plantations were the heartbeat of the rural South, galleries were for evening strolls, porches for sitting on rainy days, and verandas for sipping mint juleps on lazy summer afternoons.

What keeps the South alive today are people like Jean Boyer and Arnold Hymel.

"One of the great gifts the elderly can give us is a sense of roots," Jean said. "By sharing their stories, they remind us that family is what makes life worth living."

PHOTO BY JEAN BOYER

Bruce and Julie with Arnold Hymel of Norco, Louisiana.
Hymel shared his stories of the Old South.

The Big Picture

There is something in human beings that can be swept away by natural disaster, disappointment, poverty, and violence. But there is also a positive force within that pushes the perimeters of loss—inviting the heart to become bigger, more expanded. By choosing to see differently, a crisis becomes an initiation into something greater.

Pasta Party on the Prairie

With Thanksgiving just around the corner, puffing and strutting like a big fat turkey, focusing on being grateful comes
easily—just what we Americans do when the leaves turn
color and the temperature falls.

However, gratitude has much to offer the year around.
It's like Super Glue. When applied, gratitude is what holds
us tightly to one another when the whole world seems to be
falling apart. It's a vital ingredient, like the commercial "Got
Milk?"—"Got Gratitude?"

"The people of Grand Forks, North Dakota, were looking for a way to let the country know we're here," said
Marge Newark, who was telling the story. "So in January
1997, a small group of community-minded citizens, along
with the Chamber of Commerce, formed the 20-20 Committee to envision where Grand Forks could be in the year
2020."

Since North Dakota grows a large percentage of the
world's wheat, the Grand Forks folks decided to throw a
"Grand Pasta Party on the Prairie." They were hoping to
draw national attention in a yummy way.

Little did they know that Mother Nature was about to
throw them a crummy curve ball. Inadvertently, the vision-
aries of Grand Forks achieved part of their goal.

After a winter of record-breaking snowfall, about the
first of April the Red River began to rise, threatening the

114

twin towns of Grand Forks, North Dakota, and East Grand Forks, Minnesota, communities divided by the river. Men, women, and children worked around the clock, piling sandbags in an effort to beat the raging floodwaters. It couldn't be done.

By April 19, the entire population of the two towns was evacuated—first by car, then by National Guard trucks, rowboats, and rescue helicopters. The good news is that no one died in the disaster. The bad news is that many lost their homes and all their belongings.

In public shelters and homes of strangers, evacuees huddled together like refugees, shivering and numb, as they helplessly watched the national news and saw their cars, pickups, and lawn furniture float down the muddy river. The river reached a record high of 54.1 feet, more than twenty-six feet above flood level. They worried and wondered. What was left of their community?

"My daughter's family and I drove to Minot, North Dakota, about two hundred miles northwest, and camped out at a motel. We were fairly comfortable though we ached for all those who were in shelters and had lost their entire homes," Marge told us.

In Minot, Marge volunteered at the Red Cross, answering phone calls from people around the country who wanted to help. Amid the chill of disaster, the wealth of assistance was heartwarming. Big boxes of clothing, tons of food, ample medical supplies, thousands of caring volunteers, truckloads of blankets, and fifteen million dollars from an anonymous donor called "The Angel" poured into the area.

After several weeks of roaring, the river quieted and began its slow recession. People began trickling back to see how grim their situation was. There was no potable water, no heat, no electricity. Some lost everything. Others just had wet basements.

But the people were not defeated.

Marge came back to her home on May 5. "As we began to get our lives back in order, to redesign our future as a city once again, we decided to continue our 20-20 vision," Marge said. "We would move forward with the plans for the 'Pasta Party on the Prairie,' but now it would be a grand 'Thank You' party to show our gratitude to the people of America and to the whole world who showered us with love."

The *Life* magazine photographers who covered the devastation of the flood returned in late August to snap a wide-angled community photo of the flood survivors as they celebrated at the national event: The Grand Pasta Party on the Prairie.

Thousands of pasta lovers swung to the music of live entertainment, listened to local and state speakers publicly thank the nation, and gazed with awe at the heavenly late-night, laser-light show.

Though the flood is over, the tears of gratitude are still flowing.

President Jimmy Carter

Smoosh. I bit into a slippery boiled peanut. Not knowing what to expect, I made a face.

"I guess you have to acquire a taste for them," said the clerk at the Golden Peanut Company, formerly the Carter family warehouse.

Thank goodness, we stopped in Plains, Georgia, not to satisfy a hunger for boiled peanuts but to feed our growing appetite for American history.

Plains is like Andy Griffith's Mayberry. Not a bush or picket fence has been changed in thirty years. On Main Street, we snapped pictures of the old train depot—President Jimmy Carter's 1976 campaign headquarters—and his brother Billy's service station.

Jimmy Carter, once known as "Jimmy Who?" in national politics, graduated from Plains High School in 1941. He attended the U.S. Naval Academy and served in the nuclear submarine program. After his father died, he returned to Plains to manage the family farm business.

Later, he entered the Georgia Senate and in 1970 became the governor.

Nobody, however, thought even the most educated peanut farmer would become President of the United States. Few candidates from the South had achieved this in more than one hundred years.

But Jimmy Carter did. And when he did, his whole rural community rented a train and came to Washington to celebrate. While Carter was in office, his high school class had a barbecue at the White House, a special class reunion. The Carters never forgot their humble beginnings.

We sat teary-eyed, watching a twenty-minute movie in the old Plains High School auditorium. The squeaky wooden chairs and echoing beige walls reminded me of my elementary school in rural Indiana. The film, pieced together from old photos and narrated by Charles Kuralt, oozed with patriotic pride.

"History will be the final judge," Kuralt said. "Carter was inaugurated in the aftermath of Watergate. The country needed a man of integrity, and the people chose Carter."

Kuralt spoke of Carter's accomplishments: the Alaska national parks, the Strategic Arms Limitation Treaty, the energy bill, and the 1978 peace agreement that Carter brought between Israeli Prime Minister Menachem Begin and Egyptian President Anwar Sadat at Camp David.

However, in 1980 when Carter was not reelected, the family came home, stinging from defeat. But the people of Plains knew what to do. They had the world's largest potluck dinner to welcome them.

"It was raining," said Kuralt. "Even the sky was weeping for Jimmy Carter."

In 1996 Plains High School was renovated and opened as a part of the National Park Service. Near the front entrance to the old brick school hangs a picture of Miss Julia Coleman, school principal, who often said, "Who knows? Maybe one of you will become President of the United States."

At the visitors' desk we met volunteer Virginia Harris Williams, one of Jimmy's classmates.

"We think he was spared another term," she said. "He's done so much good since then."

We returned on Sunday morning to attend Carter's Sunday school class and find out. The pastor of Maranatha Baptist Church introduced the thirty-ninth president.

"He's not what I would call a religious person. He's a person of faith. He lives what he believes," he said.

"If you are a visitor, please stand," said the former president. As hundreds of people from around the world stood tall, Carter's face broke into a smile as wide as the state of Georgia. "Please shout out where you are from," he invited. People said Colorado, Indiana, South Dakota, India, and others. "Ohio," Bruce and I said loudly.

Before beginning the class, Carter rattled off a brief update on his week's activities in Atlanta at the Carter Center. He spoke with high regard of a group working with troubled teens in Georgia. A delegation was sent to Uganda. Another team is resolving a leadership crisis in Zaire. And a delegation is in Libya helping the two-thirds of the citizens who are displaced, many as refugees.

Wow! Jimmy and Rosalynn Carter could be playing golf all day but instead are making the world a better place for our grandchildren.

Carter teaches Sunday school two, and sometimes three, times a month. And he's not afraid to roll up his sleeves. Every June the Carters hammer nails at the annual Jimmy Carter Work Project, a Habitat for Humanity blitz build (Call 1-800-HABITAT to volunteer).

After church we stood in line to have our picture taken with the Carters—American heroes we could get our arms around.

Habitat Builds New Lives

Hattie Pitts says the message of Habitat is life. Then Hattie, wearing a purple silk blouse and a white baseball cap, pauses and rolls her shining brown eyes skyward.

"Habitat brought me from nobody to somebody. I was living in a three-room, raggedy house, no bathroom. If I asked my landlord to fix the house, he would raise my rent," she said.

Like 70,000 Habitat homeowners, Hattie had little hope of ever escaping the poverty trap. However, she was living in Americus, a small town in southwest Georgia, where in 1976 Linda and Millard Fuller launched Habitat for Humanity International, a nonprofit, affordable housing project. By 1995 Habitat was the twentieth largest home builder in the United States.

Unique to Habitat, houses are built in teams by volunteers of all ages from diverse backgrounds. Out of the 350 people working at the international headquarters, one-third are volunteers, and many are Habitat homeowners.

Thirteen years ago, Hattie applied for an interest-free loan on a twenty-year Habitat mortgage. Then, like all qualifying homeowners, she pounded nails, sanded floors, and painted walls, putting in five hundred hours of sweat equity. Her cheerful attitude paid off. Two years later, she was offered a job as the Habitat Homeowner Coordinator.

"At first I thought Carol was offering me a custodial job. But when she said it was a desk job, I said, 'No-o-o-o,'" Hattie said.

But the woman on the other end of the line, who knew Hattie as a friend, persisted. "Come in on Friday morning. And stop saying 'no,'" she said.

Hattie hung up the phone and started crying. "The closer it got to Friday, the more worried I got," she said.

On Friday morning Carol strolled Hattie around the Habitat offices, introducing her as if the deed were done. At the end of the receiving line, Hattie grabbed Carol's arm and pulled her aside.

"Carol, I'm not taking the job," she whispered.

"I'm hiring you today, Hattie," Carol insisted. "You can do this job."

"Put me on a trial basis," Hattie pleaded.

When Carol refused, Hattie broke down in tears. "Carol, I can't read that well," she said.

Carol brushed it off like sand with a broom. "No problem. I'll give you a Dictaphone," she said.

Back at home, Hattie cried again. "I didn't know what a Dictaphone was," she said, shaking her head. "That was twelve years ago. I never held a Dictaphone in my hand."

Instead, she enrolled in a vocational school where she studied basic reading and math. Her life fell into place except one thing: her relationship with her friends.

"When I got into my Habitat house, I lost all my friends. Sometimes these things happen. I can't say what it is. Maybe it's about breaking the poverty cycle," she said, wrinkling her brow. Then smiling, she added, "It can be broken. I just needed a listening ear, and Habitat provided that."

Today, the one listening is Hattie. It's her job. Each year she visits some 260 Sumter County Habitat homeowners.

"I let them know we care, and I remind them that they may have to deal with a lot to keep their house. Things come up that you aren't planning on. Kids get sick, husbands can leave, people die—things that can happen in any household," she said.

Sometimes Hattie has to dig deep into her own experience to help those who fall short on courage. Wagging her finger, she said, "I tell them, 'I am fifty-four years old, my husband left me with six children—I do know what you are going through. I had to fight to keep from going back to poverty. And I did it, by the grace of God.'"

In addition, she just received an award for her after-school reading program. Today, Hattie—the one who had little confidence in her ability to read—leads thirty-one children in getting the skills she missed.

"Millard always tells us, 'We are not only building houses. We also build lives, and that is really true," she said. "And that's my life."

To find out more about Habitat, call 1-800-HABITAT.

The Civil Rights Memorial

In 1954 the U.S. Supreme Court outlawed segregation in schools, triggering a magnitude of violence and white terrorist activity that ran rampant as wildfire throughout the Deep South. Between 1954 and 1968, black and many sympathetic white citizens were beaten, murdered, lynched, and assassinated by white men who considered Negroes unworthy of the rights promised them by the Constitution.

We stood in silence at the Civil Rights Memorial in front of the Southern Poverty Law Center in Montgomery, Alabama. Our fingers mingled in the stream of water flowing from the center of a circular black granite table that records the names of forty heroes who lost their lives in the struggle for equality. On a curved black granite wall behind the table are engraved the biblical words quoted by Dr. Martin Luther King, Jr.—"We will not be satisfied, 'until justice rolls down like waters and righteousness like a mighty stream.'"

There were many visitors that day: students from a Texas university, a Methodist youth group from Iowa, a couple from Italy, and a black woman with tears in her eyes, standing as if guarding the tomb of a lost son.

In 1955 the Reverend George Lee, one of the first black registered voters in Humphrey County, Mississippi, was murdered because he refused to stop working toward voter registration. Lamar Smith, a sixty-three-year-old World War II

124

veteran, was shot dead by a white man in broad daylight. No one would testify. That same year, Rosa Parks was arrested for refusing to give up her seat on a bus to a white man. This began the Montgomery bus boycott that drew Dr. King, a Baptist minister, into the fight for freedom.

In November 1956, the Supreme Court banned segregated seating on Montgomery buses, but the inequalities and the killing didn't stop. John Earl Reese, sixteen, was slain by nightriders (drive-by killers) opposed to black school improvements. Willie Edwards Jr., twenty-three, drowned when he was forced to jump from a bridge by Ku Klux Klansmen who were out to kill a black man that night. They did. And Mack Charles Parker, twenty-three, accused of raping a white woman, was assumed guilty, taken from jail, and lynched by an angry white mob.

None of the victims was armed, and none of the killers was indicted. That was justice, Southern style.

The victims of discrimination grew during the 1960s to include white civil rights workers and teens. William Lewis Moore, a white postman from Baltimore, was shot and killed during a march against segregation. In 1964 "Freedom Summer" brought over one thousand civil rights volunteers to Mississippi. James Earl Chaney, a black youth, Andrew Goodman and Michael Schwerner, white youths, were arrested by a deputy sheriff and then released into the hands of Klansmen who had methodically plotted their murders.

The following year, King, by now a leading inspirational speaker and advocate of nonviolent desegregation, brought to Selma the power and attention of national media. However, the growing numbers of white supremacists were not threatened by the increase in outsiders. James Reeb, a Unitarian minister from Boston and one of the many white clergy who flew to Alabama to join the Selma-to-Montgomery march, was beaten to death on a Selma street. And Viola Gregg Liuzzo, a housewife and mother from Detroit who helped transport blacks during the Selma march, was shot and killed by Klansmen from a passing car.

In response to the Selma March, Congress passed the Voting Rights Act on July 9, 1965, outlawing obstacles to black voting. Federal officials were empowered to enforce the legislation.

How is this a bountiful story? The Civil Rights Memorial is not about suffering. It is a memorial of hope, designed by Maya Lin, who is also the architect of the Vietnam Memorial. Its aim is to remind us in a majestic yet simple way that the cause of freedom must continue to flow. Inequality in housing, education, job opportunities, and health care are ongoing concerns of a democratic society. Though we have come far in the quest for equality, the story of intolerance in America is far from over.

The Southern Poverty Law Center

"In America we have the right to hate, but not hurt," says Morris Dees, executive director of the Southern Poverty Law Center in Montgomery, Alabama. But walking that fine line requires more than justice. It takes guts.

In 1971 Dees was determined to continue the work of the Civil Rights Movement. Dees, who grew up in Montgomery, organized a small group of attorneys to serve the underdog, victims of civil rights atrocities and those who survived them.

Today, the nonprofit law center that operates solely on private donations is internationally known for its legal victories against white supremacist groups, and for Teaching Tolerance, an extension of the center's educational effort to prevent violence.

Armed guards swarm like honeybees outside the Southern Poverty Law Center. Why? Because in 1983 the center was firebombed by Ku Klux Klansmen. In the guardhouse we were asked why we wanted to visit the law offices. Generally, tourists come to see the Civil Rights Memorial, which was sponsored by the center in 1989 and is located directly in front of the law building.

Without a *Sun* newspaper press card to flash, we simply shared our journey of hope. It worked. Like Dorothy being graciously welcomed to the Emerald City of Oz, we were escorted up the steps and into the contemporary building full of angles and light.

"We monitor the activity of hate groups, " said our tour guide, gesturing to a wall map forested with pushpins. Each point represents a pocket of anti-something activity in the U.S.

"Look at Ohio," whispered Bruce, rolling his eyes. A cold chill ran down my spine as I counted the hot spots.

"We publish information about their activity in our magazine, *KLANWATCH*," she said, handing us a copy.

On the cover of *KLANWATCH*, a militia group touting a Confederate flag prepared for war. White neo-Nazi skinheads—their right arms raised in a stiff salute, eyes glazed, teeth set in rage, arteries bulging—were ready to release their venom. I cringed.

That evening I read several eye-opening stories. One opened my heart. In the spring of 1981, two Klansmen heard on the 10:00 P.M. news that the jury in a case of a black man charged with the murder of a white policeman was dead-locked. Angered, they decided to kill a black man that night. Any black man.

Armed with a .22-caliber pistol and a rope tied in a hangman's noose, James Knowles, seventeen, and Henry Hayes, twenty-six, drove to a black neighborhood and found Michael Donald, nineteen, a masonry student at Carver State Technical College and the youngest son of Beulah Mae Donald. They beat him, cut his throat, and hanged him from a tree.

Despite the evidence, the district attorney said that neither race nor Klan activity seemed to be factors in the death.

When one thousand blacks marched in protest, Dees, like Luke Skywalker wielding his light saber, stepped into action and helped Beulah Mae and the NAACP file a civil suit against the United Klans of America. Never before had the Klan been held responsible for its policy of violence.

The force was with them. The multimillion dollar judgment bankrupted that Klan faction, the first in a series of victories Dees would have over tyrannical hate groups. However, Dees says the real victory came after that first trial, when Knowles, who plea bargained and was sentenced to life, asked to make a closing statement.

"I've lost my family, and I've got people after me," said the seventeen-year-old. "I was acting as a Klansman. I hope people learn from my mistake, learn what it cost me."

Then he turned to Beulah Mae and told her that he had nothing to pay her, but if it took the rest of his life to make amends, he would. Sobbing, he asked if she could find it in her heart to forgive him.

With tears in her eyes, she softly said, "I have already forgiven you."

Learning doesn't have to be so hard. Teaching Tolerance's award-winning curriculum materials that promote interracial and intercultural understanding are free to teachers. Teachers may fax requests on their school letterhead to (334) 264-3121.

8

Unsolved Mysteries

At some obscure mile marker, let's say around 20,000 miles into our journey of hope, the spirit of adventure reached right out of the U.S. map and grabbed my soul. No longer would two-week-vacation-gulps to Florida suffice. After crisscrossing scores of state lines, our appetite for what makes America AMERICA jumped off the charts. There was so much to learn and see—some of which we could never fully understand, but no longer did that count.

Disillusionment Brings New Light

The McDonald Observatory, located near the town of Fort Davis, in west Texas, is perched 6,800 feet atop Mount Locke in the heart of the Davis Mountains. Astronomers from around the globe sign up on a waiting list—sometimes years in advance—and then pray for good weather so that they can use the acclaimed research facility.

We took the forty-five-minute orientation tour, beginning with a breathtaking climb up seventy-some steps to the white-domed observatory room where the giant 107-inch Harlan J. Smith telescope is housed.

"There is no lens in this telescope. It's not for seeing pretty things. The nine-foot-diameter mirror gathers and reflects starlight," said our tour guide, a man in his mid-forties with a balding head surrounded by wiry-gray hair. He looked like the quintessential mad scientist.

"We are doing science," he said with dead seriousness. "Everything we see in the universe can be explained in terms of math, physics, and chemistry. There are no miracles. It's the same everywhere, the same ninety-two elements. Earth is not unique in the universe."

Thirty-some other spectators were glassy-eyed. A few were yawning, but my mind was screaming, "What about possibility, humility, spirituality, and childlike curiosity?"

How odd that a world-famous observatory, a massive monument to the beyond, would be void of wonder. Had it slid out the window like a falling star? And why was our tour guide so decided about life, almost cynical? Where was his playful inner child?

We returned that evening for the "Star Party," a guided observation of the night sky. When we arrived, however, the sky was overcast with a raggedy umbrella of clouds. In the distance, bolts of lighting whirled their fiery wands. Our spirits slumped. Would there be stargazing tonight?

Our evening tour guide, a man in his early thirties, dressed in L. L. Bean shorts and a *Star Trek* T-shirt, greeted us with a bright smile and reassuring news. With the aid of computers, there would be a star party.

"In a planetarium, you can customize the sky, look at the stars when you were born, take the mouse and click on the moon, and get important information. Computer programs are wonderful!" he said with contagious enthusiasm.

We gazed at Corvus, the Raven, Scorpius with its long body, stinger, and tail, Lyra's graceful harp, and the bold Northern Cross. Soon our interest in astronomy and the wonders of science was restored.

Though much of science is predictable, there are some things that defy explanation. Just twenty-one miles south of Fort Davis, in the tiny town of Marfa, Texas, there have been reports of mysterious lights for nearly two hundred years. Scientists have tried to explain this strange phenomenon, but they have no answers.

Nine miles east of Marfa at Paisano Pass, carloads of curious spectators gather nightly to observe the moving, unidentified lights in the distance. The next day, we drove out at dusk to see for ourselves.

Sure enough, two lights appeared, split into four glowing balls, got brighter, then dimmer, and disappeared. When they reappeared a few minutes later, the dance continued.

Later in the week, we were sitting in an outdoor amphitheater eagerly waiting for the Park Ranger to explain the importance of bats at Carlsbad Caverns National Park (southeast corner of New Mexico). We stumbled upon a scene there that shed some light on the lifeless "mad scientist" we had met earlier.

A three-year-old boy, wearing a red baseball cap and matching red sneakers, squirmed on the bench as his mother told a story about him to a woman who sat behind them.

"When I asked Jeffrey how he was after an hour of driving, he said, 'George and I are fine, Mom.'" Raising her eyebrows, she explained, "George is Jeffrey's imaginary friend."

With that bit of ammunition, Jeffrey's seven- and nine-year-old siblings began taunting him. The child's arms went limp, and tiny tears dripped down his face. Then, like a big bear protecting a little cub, the father scooped the boy onto his knee and said, "I had an imaginary friend when I was your age." The child's eyes lit up again.

If we had all the answers, there would be no science, no inquiry into the great unknown, and no tomorrow for the child within.

Alabama Burning

Visiting Boligee, Alabama, has made us a little smarter, a wee more humble, and a lot more inquisitive as bounty hunters.

You may recall the burning of more than seventy black churches in the South in 1996–97 and how it brought national attention, federal investigation, and help from thousands of volunteers—mainly Quakers, Mennonites, and Unitarians—eager to take a stand against social and racial injustice. This was our kind of story.

However, after two disappointing interviews, we suspected something was amiss. Mount Zion Baptist Church was originally a modest, frame structure on a dusty country road in Greene County. The ten-member church burned to the ground on December 22, 1995. Replacing it today is a solid brick building with stained glass windows. It's nice, but it's not enough.

"All those good memories got burned up," said Annie B. Watkins, longtime church member.

Although Annie was deeply touched by the people who helped rebuild the church, she fears that arsonists could torch it again—"the next time with people in the church," she said.

Rebuilding churches may not solve deeper problems.

Twenty minutes later, we sat on a front porch enjoying the warm April sun and visiting with Miss Courtney Porter, longtime member of Little Zion Baptist Church. This historic church was founded by slaves two hundred years ago in rural Alabama. On January 11, 1996, the eve of Martin Luther King Day, it was burned. The small congregation was shocked.

"In slavery times, this was the richest county. Now it's the poorest. That tells you something," Miss Porter said with raised eyebrows. But she didn't say what.

Outside the Boligee Café, we questioned a local man about his feelings.

"Don't quote me," he said, sidestepping into how much money was raised and how it was spent, "but one church even has air conditioning now." He spoke as if reporting something he thinks the few-membered church cannot possibly afford.

Why did so few people in the community reach out? The man couldn't say, but directed us to someone who could—Marilyn Cork.

On the way to meet Marilyn, we drove by Mount Zoar Baptist Church, the third sparkling-new church on a remote country road. Like the others, it was rebuilt of fireproof bricks.

Unlike the others, it was wrapped in a wrought iron fence. From behind locked gates the church looked more like a strange prison than a house of worship.

"After it burned. I drove by the rubble, mainly to see where the church was," said Marilyn. "Then I realized it wasn't right just to drive by."

So she rallied her church in nearby Eutaw, Alabama, to fix meals that summer for the volunteers, mostly Mennonite teenagers and young adults. On July Fourth Marilyn made a hand-decorated cake as a reminder to the group to celebrate.

We arrived in Boligee expecting to find good things and certainly we did. The churches were rebuilt, there were glowing reports about the people who rebuilt them, and blacks and whites of many faiths had worked together all summer.

Yet the silence was screaming: "There is more work to be done in Greene County."

Two weeks later, Marilyn called to tell us more.

"It's not real positive," she warned us, knowing our never-ending quest for good news. "Greene County has been in the national news for more than burning churches." She referred to two articles about political corruption and vote fraud covered in *Reader's Digest* (July 1996) and *The National Review* (June 17, 1996).

We jumped in the truck and headed for a library. Sure enough, in 1994, 34 percent of the all ballots in Greene County were cast absentee. According to Alabama's Secretary of State, absentee ballots should account for only three or four percent of all votes cast.

Others were said to have voted under the threat that if they didn't cooperate, they would lose their public assistance. According to *The National Review*, "In destitute Greene County, Alabama, democracy is practiced strictly Third World-style by the local black Democratic machine."

Bing. A light flipped on. Had the national news covering the sacrilege of burning churches taken the heat off voting fraud?

136

At the end of June, *USA Today* reported the findings of a two-month investigation of church fires across the South. There was no evidence of a widespread racial conspiracy, and racial hatred was found to be only one of many motives behind the fires.

Was voting fraud one of them? We don't know. But perhaps we missed the best story in Boligee—about the Citizens for a Better Greene County, a group focused on "honest elections, truth, and accountability in government."

Enchanted in New Mexico

The sun shines so brightly in New Mexico that the sky appears to be brush-stroked deep azure, and the earth seems to be sculpted in rusty reds and golden acrylic browns.

It's the light that has let New Mexico become known as the Land of Enchantment. And it's why artists flock to Albuquerque, Taos, and Santa Fe. They come to capture the essence of vibrant color on canvas and through the camera.

Ultimately, the enchantment of New Mexico captures their souls, as it did ours.

In Albuquerque's Old Town Plaza, street merchants sell their Indian art year-round on blankets spread on sidewalks under heavy awnings. They offer corn necklaces in bright pink and emerald green, silver earrings with turquoise stones, beaded bracelets, dreamcatchers, and hand-painted coyotes wearing bright bandanas as they howl at the moon. Prices are astonishingly reasonable, and there's no sales tax.

Some 120 miles north of Albuquerque, in Taos, the galleries along Paseo del Pueblo Norte are stocked full of art on consignment. It's a good thing browsing is my favorite sport.

But the truly impressive area is found behind the commercial shops on Ledoux Street, where artists Ernest and Mary Blumenschein's former adobe studio-home is today a museum and National Historic Landmark. The Blumenscheins, who moved to Taos from Paris in 1912, are two of the six original founders of the Taos Society of Artists.

The Navaho Gallery of R. C. Gorman is also a favorite on Ledoux. Gorman's use of brilliant color depicting Navaho women in everyday postures is his way of honoring the sacredness of his people.

Another kind of New Mexico light draws ordinary people to kneel in prayer at famous chapels and churches, all built when the territory was being settled by Spanish-speaking Roman Catholics.

North and east of Santa Fe is the village of Chimayo. There, in a small chapel built in 1816, big miracles have occurred. El Santuario de Chimayo is today a legendary shrine. Stories, handwritten and framed for tourists to read, tell of healings and cures related to the sprinkling of sacred sand found in the small room behind the altar. Discarded crutches and braces bear testimony to the power of faith that attracts visitors from far away.

In Santa Fe, we stopped at the Chapel of Our Lady of Light to see the Inexplicable Stairs, built for the sisters whose prayers were answered by a carpenter named Joseph.

In September 1852, the Sisters of Loretto came up the Mississippi River from Kentucky and across the plains and south to New Mexico to form a community in Santa Fe. Because they are a teaching order, they needed a school. Soon the school was built by Mexican carpenters.

Next, they needed a chapel, to be designed after the bishop's fancy Sainte Chapelle in Paris, a gothic structure. But the French and Italian masons who worked on the chapel forgot one vital piece of the architecture: the staircase to the choir loft.

This was a big problem. If built as an afterthought, the stairs would dominate the entire structure, destroying its delicate beauty. The sisters, not willing to change their plans, decided to ask for divine assistance. After all, what is a great church without at least one good miracle and a dose of faith?

The sisters began to say a novena dedicated to their patron saint, St. Joseph. According to the legend, on the last day of the one-month-long prayer, a gray-haired man named Joseph came to the convent with a donkey and a toolbox and asked Mother Magdalene, the sister in charge, if he could help with the stairs. I have a hunch she smiled and said yes.

It is said that the only tools Joseph had were a hammer, a saw, and a T-square. He worked with wood that to this day is identified as not-local, soaking each piece in water before cutting it.

Eight months later, Joseph finished his work of art— the circular staircase that has two complete 360-degree turns. Amazingly, there was no banister and no supporting center pole in the finished product. Only wooden pegs held it together.

When Sister Magdalene went to pay Joseph, he had gone.

The staircase, used daily for over one hundred years, defies all laws of gravity, according to modern-day architects. Though some say it's a fluke, the sisters are sure their prayers were answered.

An Angel at the BC Ranch

Becky Smith and Cathy Fortenberry are the owners of the BC Ranch, located along Highway 118 north of Alpine, Texas. In 1981, Perry Cartwright bequeathed the 5,000-acre ranch to Smith, an R.N.-turned-cowgirl, because he knew she would keep the ranch, not sell it to developers. He also knew she would treat the purebred Herefords with tender loving care, as his family did for over one hundred years.

What Cartwright couldn't know is that the ranch would become a kind of Texas Field of Dreams.

For the last eighteen autumns, during roundup, when additional hands are needed, the BC Ranch transforms into a dude ranch for women—volunteers who come from various backgrounds to embrace the spirit of ranching. For many this is the fulfillment of a lifelong dream.

For three power-packed days, fifteen or more women, using no whips, no spurs, and no cattle prods—just lots of whoops and hollers—tromp the open range on horseback, sweeping about 150 head of cattle into chutes to be tested for pregnancy, vaccinated, and wormed.

When the marathon of muscles is over, Becky and Cathy are left to carry on. Like rodeo riders gripping the reins of the last frontier, they go the distance, tending the daily chores for the rest of the year—mending fences, digging ditches, and repairing vehicles.

Two years ago they built an RV park on a few frontage acres, hoping to bridge the gap between fickle beef prices and rising expenses. Otherwise, they didn't know how they could keep the ranch.

But the reins snapped in 1996 when Cathy lost her leg due to a blood clot. The robust woman, who grew up on a Texas farm and took to ranching like a calf to its mother, had no choice. An above-the-knee amputation of her left leg saved her life and changed it forever.

Lying immobilized on a cold hospital gurney, Cathy worried. How would she care for herself, let alone hold up her partnership in the ranch and the new RV park?

"During the surgery," she said, "someone—an angel dressed in a gray-and-black-striped baseball uniform, wearing a baseball glove on his left hand—came to ease my pain."

"He patted me on the shoulder, told me that everything was going to be all right, and waved at me as I left the operating room," Cathy told us. "He had only one leg."

She added, "The experience left me with such a sense of well-being, but it would have made more sense if the angel were someone like Chester from the TV show *Gunsmoke*. I don't know anything about sports."

But after talking to a knowledgeable friend, she found it did make sense. Monty Stratton, five-year pitcher for the Chicago White Sox, was raised on a farm in west Texas. His baseball career was shortened in 1938 when he lost his right leg in a hunting accident at his mother's farm, not far from the BC Ranch. Stratton, then the leading right-handed pitcher in the American League, was devastated.

But not for long. With a wooden leg and a lot of determination, Stratton became a pitching coach, and in 1946 he startled the world when he began pitching again for the Chicago White Sox. His comeback was the subject of a 1949 Metro-Goldwyn-Mayer film, *The Stratton Story,* starring James Stewart, June Allyson, and Agnes Moorehead.

Though Stratton died in 1982 at the age of seventy, baseball heroes of exceptional courage keep batting. Remember, the ghost players in the movie *Field of Dreams* were members of the White Sox.

In the weeks and months that followed the surgery, Cathy struggled to accept her loss and to learn to walk with a prosthesis. Many times she felt the low ebb of despair and the restless high of panic.

"Then I'd hear this little voice coaching me to get a hold of myself," she said. "I swear to God it was Stratton."

In the movie *Field of Dreams* people came from miles to visit the Iowa cornfield, to hit a few baseballs, and to reminisce about their favorite sport, baseball. Likewise, we hope people will also come to the BC Ranch RV park where they can watch the cattle roam and remember yesterday's cowboys and the Wild West.

Don't Worry, Be Hopi

We are on the road, heading for the Hopi Reservation to meet Joe and Janice Day, who live in Second Mesa, Arizona, 6,000 feet high on a mountain plateau (mesa). From Holbrook, Arizona, it's a seventy-mile trek north through the Painted Desert, past mountains of golden yellow stone and oceans of powder-green sage brush.

As we drive, we begin to wonder: Are we looking to Native American customs for answers? Or are we learning the importance of customs and traditions from those who never gave them up?

Near the mesa the Ford shifts gears, working hard to climb the switchback road. How quickly the land becomes flat again, for mesa is Spanish for *table,* and we had reached the top. I searched in my purse for the directions, scribbled on a scrap of paper. "It's one-and-a half miles east of the Hopi Cultural Center on Highway 264," I said. Then I spelled the name of the Days' trading post: TSAKURSHOVI, for I could not pronounce it.

Two minutes later, we stepped into the cozy two-room adobe trading post. My eyes quickly spied the well-stocked jewelry cases, filled with handmade treasures: turquoise and silver pins, beaded barrettes, and earrings decked with polished stones. Gazing up, I was captured by dozens of colorful Kachina dolls suspended from the white stucco walls.

Then, bright-lettered words printed in gold on a navy blue sweatshirt caught my attention: DON'T WORRY, BE HOPI. A man of medium height with thick gray hair and a friendly smile reached across the counter to shake hands. His name was Joe Day.

Joe, fifty-four, grew up in Witchita, Kansas, and Middletown, Ohio. Today, he is married to Janice, a member of the Bear Strap Clan. Their modern home next to the trading post offers a stunning view of the desert and mesas in all directions.

"Women follow their mother's clan when they marry, and men follow their wives'," instructed Joe, who refers to himself as a *bahana*, the Hopi term for Anglo.

We proceeded to ask several questions. "*Bahanas* ask a lot of questions," Joe said. "They categorize, analyze, and even try to make sense of what takes a lifetime to understand."

Janice was shopping in Flagstaff that day, ninety miles away, so Joe offered to be our tour guide. The pickup bumped along from mesa to mesa as Joe pointed out the different Hopi villages, thirteen in all, atop three mesas on the reservation. How soon the sun began its descent, casting a dazzling-white glow on the mountaintops. Joe invited us to return in the morning.

Just then, Janice pulled into the driveway in a sporty red pickup. When she saw Bruce's sunburned face, she ran for the remedy—aloe. Her straight black hair shone in the evening light as we waved good-bye.

In the morning, we hurried to make our phone calls and write letters, trying to get on our way to Second Mesa. Joe was right. *Bahanas* are detail-minded creatures who are much too worried!

Breathless, we arrived by mid-afternoon. Janice was patiently splitting yucca leaves to weave an initiation plaque for her godchild. Joe was ready for us with Hopi history.

Joe told us the story of Janice's uncle, Lewis Tewanima, a famous athlete who ran with Jim Thorpe in the Olympics of 1912. He told us about the Hopi Solar Energy Project and how the people are working to be more self-sufficient. And he reminded us that the Hopi have always lived on this land. Recently, the Hopi voted down casinos.

That evening, we ate dinner at the Cultural Center down the road. Janice spoke about the main concern of her people—enough rain for crops. Even in this arid land, they can grow melons, squash, corn, and beans and tend fruit orchards.

I asked if she ever feels confined living miles away from a city. "Recently, we took a trip to New York. When we returned, I wanted to kiss the land," she said with a big smile.

The next morning, we were up early and on our way to Hopiland—no fussing with letters and no phone calling. Today, we are invited to see ancient petroglyphs still visible on canyon walls. Janice greeted us with a hug, freshly brewed mugs of coffee, and an introduction to a new visitor joining us today. The new visitor was already firing up the questions. Wow, that's how we sounded only two days ago!

I recalled Joe's words, "It's okay to be *bahana*. We are pioneers. We like to see new things. We are natural-born tourists."

But our questions are not in vain. There is much to learn from ancient cultures—values core to our early American

146

culture as well: Honor the family, live in community, and think in terms of many generations. And like the Hopi— not to worry!

9

The Winning Formula

Victory comes in many forms. It may be the thrill of participating in a monumental marathon or the camaraderie of winning a state championship. It can be the warmhearted feeling that emanates when a community project brings families together for a worthy cause. But the greatest of all is victory over death. When the intention to heal the pain of death results in experiencing oneness with others, then we have truly tapped into a universal winning formula.

The Wadsworth Grizzlies

Winning the girls' basketball state championship is a big deal, especially for a small town like Wadsworth, Ohio. Recently, we asked five-foot-two senior guard, Jenny Martin for her winning formula.

"We are all best friends, and we do everything together," she said.

The Lady Grizzlies swept all but one of their Suburban League games by thirty points in 1997.

We used to talk about the games at our sleepovers," Jenny said. "We wondered what the other teams must be thinking and decided that if we ever started losing, we would keep saying, "'We are not giving up.'"

Everyone thought the Grizzlies were dribbling toward the state tournament except the girls themselves. Week after week, the teens snuggled in blankets, munched on pizzas, and sipped Cokes late at night, sharing their deepest concern.

"A few years ago, another team was slotted to go to the state games and didn't make it," Jenny said. The Grizzlies, not wanting to feel the sting of embarrassment, decided to take one game at a time. That's how they made it to the state semifinals.

"Coach [Todd] Osborn prepared us for the level of noise we'd experience at St. John Arena [in Columbus]," Jenny explained. "He had us practice with a radio blasting full static in the background. He told us to use hand motions and work as a team. We would have to find a way to communicate with one another."

Though March 14 was a cold day in Columbus, Ohio, the heat was on at St. John Arena where seven thousand fans rocked the bleachers, screaming their heads off. In the third quarter of the first playoff game, the Grizzlies trailed ten points behind the nationally ranked Pickerington Tigers. Through nail-biting tension, the Grizzlies kept fighting.

Then click. Something familiar snapped into place when sophomore Katelyn Vujas made a three-point play, giving the Grizzlies their first lead of the game. In the last few seconds, senior Kristin Hoover, the team's rebound grabber, made the winning point. Yes!

Jenny's dad, John Martin (the boys' basketball coach) added, "All coaches strive to achieve team cohesion. Some teams will just blow you off. These kids responded."

In the final game, March 15, the Wadsworth Grizzlies were losing to the Mason Comets, 46-39. With less than six minutes left to play, a Comet made a fatal blunder. As Wadsworth sophomore Kate Lyren was recovering from a tumble to the floor, a Comet ground her foot into Kate's stomach, igniting the tired Grizzlies to fever-pitch action. With fire in her eyes, Jenny sank two back-to-back three-point shots, cutting the deficit to a single point.

In the final play, Jenny delivered a pass to Kate, who made the winning basket as the buzzer went off. The Wadsworth fans rose to honor the first-time state champions, and the Lady Grizzlies fell into one big puppy pile on the gym floor, hugging and screaming for joy. Coach Osborn's constant message, "These are your sisters," was never truer.

The next day, the Wadsworth police escorted the victors down High Street to the center of town where two thousand fans waved and poked WE LOVE YOU signs in the cool air to welcome home the tired teenagers.

Though the games are over, the fame lives on. This year, the Lady Grizzlies will speak at the Wadsworth fifth-grade graduation, something a coach would normally do. Recently, a fourth grader called Jenny—to acknowledge her as "a really good player"—and to ask if she would come to his soccer game. She said, "Yes."

Another child mailed Jenny his ticket stub and the lucky penny he found at the Pickerington game. Hoping his hero would write back, he included a self-addressed envelope with a twenty-cent stamp.

"All the girls signed the ticket, and we sent it back to him," Jenny said.

Perhaps elementary school student Jessica Kleinman wrote to Jenny Martin the best summary of what a winning team means to its fans. "I'm probably your number one fan," she said. "Being around you makes me feel special."

Jenny, who wants to be an elementary school teacher, recalls years ago when she and Kate Lyren would shoot endless baskets in their backyards.

"We used to say, 'At the buzzer, you're going to win this game.' We would stagger the winning shot," said Jenny, still amazed at how it all played out.

Kokomo Radio

In 1968 Dick Bronson, a successful restaurant owner in Kokomo, Indiana, heard that radio WWKI 100.5 FM needed a disc jockey. "I can do that," he boldly told his wife.

She dared him and just a few years later, while hosting his own radio show, *Viewpoint*, Bronson was pressed to meet the real challenge. An unemployed autoworker called to ask how he was to give his family a happy holiday season when he couldn't even buy groceries.

Bronson pulled out his wallet, counted the cash, and said on the air, "I'm giving half, that's twenty bucks. Now I challenge our listeners to match that."

In one hour $1,100 was delivered in pennies, nickels, dimes, and dollars to the front door of the radio station.

The second year, with just a nudge of publicity, an avalanche of donations tumbled in—homemade brownies, handmade afghans, fine jewelry, used cars, even live chickens. This time, Bronson was the one who asked for help over the air. Jan Buechler, a housewife who had recently lost a child and was looking for a way to cradle her sorrow, was just one of those who answered the call.

The third year, Bronson received a call from a skeptic asking why they were continuing the project. "Because we care," he said, naming the annual fundraiser.

Each year, Jan, the volunteer coordinator, stretches to find ways to tie in the growing numbers of volunteers. One year she organized teams of volunteers to decorate elegant Christmas trees that go on display for two weeks at the local mall. Thousands, including busloads of nursing home residents, come from a five-county area to admire the glowing evergreens and to vote for their favorite tree by plunking pennies into buckets. Last year $4,999.90 in pennies was donated.

Held the first full weekend in December, WE CARE has developed into an annual forty-seven-hour nonstop radio/telethon broadcast where everything that is donated is auctioned off. Last year, eight hundred volunteers raised $756,000. Every dime goes to local charities that assist the underprivileged and the physically and mentally challenged individuals, all year long.

In 1986 the volunteers initiated a special project when a small doll wearing tattered clothes dropped out of a sack of donated clothing. Her extended hand and a stain of a tear on her face grabbed their hearts.

They named the doll Hope because she is hoping for a happy holiday season for everyone. At the end of the telethon each year, Hope goes up for auction. The first year she was purchased for $1,750 by a man for his Down's Syndrome child. The following year, he brought the doll back so that she could be auctioned again. Last year Hope sold for $84,000 to the employees of a large corporation.

Now, the doll is returned to the radio studio in a limousine, escorted by a police car. She has become the official WE CARE mascot.

For Bronson, who was raised in an impoverished farm situation, the desire to give goes back far. When he was twelve years old, he sawed up an old broomstick handle to make checkers for his brother for Christmas.

What do others get out of giving? Some see it as a way to get free publicity, public acknowledgment, and tax write-offs. Many participate as a part of their family tradition. Regardless, everyone likes the feel-good feeling.

"Then there's the redemptive giver," joked Bronson.

"The worst attorney in town, a man I hammer on the radio all year long because he handles the worst cases, walked into the studio, handed me the keys to his shiny red Porsche, and said, 'See, I'm not such a bad guy,'" Bronson told us.

Bronson's favorite story happened twenty years ago. An elderly woman dressed shabbily but wearing a red silk poinsettia corsage, came to the radio station to see if she could help. She asked Jan if she thought someone might like the old silk flower she wore. It was all she really had to give. Bronson kept the precious gift. He keeps it posted on his bulletin board as a daily reminder of the true gift of giving.

Then Jan, as if placing the star on top of the tree after all the lights and bulbs are perfectly hung, told her favorite story. One year after the TV cameras were all turned off and the volunteers had gone home, four little girls showed up, not properly dressed for winter. They were asking for Santa.

Jan, who is always the last helper to leave, called Bronson at home. In the meantime, she gathered up mittens, warm coats, and some toys. Luckily, Bronson who is round and jolly with graying hair, arrived in the twinkle of an eye.

Although the girls didn't see Santa that night, they experienced him when they met the spirit of Christmas, Dick Bronson.

The Original Sixteen to One Gold Mine

In January 1848, gold was discovered in abundance at Sutter's Mill, halfway between Sacramento and Lake Tahoe. The reaction was pandemic: gold fever.

Granted, there was a bit of madness, but it wasn't just California dreaming. "Gold has been found in all fifty-eight California counties, and the heydays are not over," says Mike Miller, corporate president of the Original Sixteen to One gold mine, the last operating, deep, hard-rock quartz mine in California.

High in the Sierra Mountains lies the treasure town of Alleghany, just twenty miles off famous Route 49. Outside the Sixteen to One mining office, a heavy load of snow slides off the slanted metal roof with a big thud. Inside, a propane gas stove pumps out heat while a four-month-old baby naps in a corner crib. Nearby, a teenager is being home-schooled by his mother. It's a hometown operation.

We are greeted and given a package of information to help us on our tour. The mine was established in 1896 but shut down in 1965 because the cost of mining exceeded the price of gold. In 1983 Miller, a fifth-generation Califor-nian who decided to get back to the land after witnessing the Watts riots, reopened it.

Soon after we arrived, in walks Miller—tall and lean, in his fifties, his hair tucked beneath a rabbitskin hat. We chat for a while, then pull on our mining attire: tall rubber boots and bright yellow hard hats.

"You're going to get the $500 tour because you are going with me," Miller said. "Let's just pretend we are going to work."

At the mining operations center, Jason, the mining engineer, is perched at the computer, studying an AutoCAD map. "This is a thinking man's mine," Miller said, walking us to a wall-size diagram that showed the mine's underground workings. "It's not just one vein. We move out in many levels."

Ian, the mine superintendent who has total responsibility for all the property, welcomes us and tells Miller, "We're gaining on it."

Miller's eyes light up like the Cheshire cat's.

"The property has only been twenty percent explored," Miller said. "So far the mine has produced 1.1 million ounces of gold in 101 years."

We rode a quarter mile to the mine entrance in a "crummy," a 4x4 vehicle that relishes bathing in thick silt mud. At the shop we geared up to go underground. Headlights are snapped onto hard hats, and leather belts, holstering a five-pound battery wired to the headlight, are wrapped around our hips. Like John Wayne, the men tromp to the mine entrance. Like Daffy Duck, I waddle behind, rubber boots too big, the bill of my hard hat over my eyes.

We follow the tram tracks into the main shaft and begin the long march to what feels like the belly of the mine, the ballroom. It's dark, damp, drippy, and dead silent.

But my mind is screaming, *"Where's the pay dirt?"* I imagine the joy that must have resonated in these underground tunnels on the million-dollar day, December 17, 1993. I feel the excitement that raced through these halls in August of 1995, when a two-million-dollar vein was struck—white quartz rock threaded with gleaming 22-carat gold. Was the thrill the same or bigger when they hit another bonanza in 1997?

"The gold is there. You just have to find it," Miller said.

It's hard work, not like buying a lottery ticket. Though today's miners use metal detectors, ground penetrating radar, and radio imaging technology, the real job still requires getting dirty. Dressed in muddy overalls worthy of a detergent commercial, the miners use dynamite followed by muscle, tunneling about six linear feet a day. These guys are the experts. When the hoist breaks down, they have to fix it.

But they have something going for them—a fearless leader who believes the mine can stand on its own through mining, not stock sales. Miller isn't dressed in a three-piece suit. He's right in there getting dirty. There is a dazzling incentive: The men get a percentage of the take!

Miller came to rural California seeking not only gold but also the spirit of the old forty-niners. He believes that spirit lives today in his miners: "Optimism, resourcefulness, and a willingness to work hard and take risks. That's old California," he said.

RAGBRAI

If you want to define Iowa, you must know about RAGBRAI. Hunting for human bounty in that state, we discovered it's what Iowa is all about.

Each summer RAGBRAI (Register's Annual Great Bike Ride Across Iowa) brings Iowans and bike enthusiasts from around the world together for a week under the golden Iowa sun. As the name says, it's sponsored by the *Des Moines Register*, the state's largest newspaper.

Now twenty-three years old, RAGBRAI is more than a tour. It's a homecoming.

Starting in Onawa in the west and pedaling day by day across the width of the Hawkeye State, ten thousand bikers spend the night in six host towns. Town residents plan activities, prepare food, find space to accommodate thousands of tents, provide entertainment, and offer open-arm support for sun-scorched bikers.

The average daily route is seventy miles. This year, 1995, the toughest day is the fourth, a ninety-eight-mile trek to the twin towns of Tama and Toledo. Lakeview, Iowa, the smallest host town, has the greatest challenge. Its population is 1,303, while its guest list is ten thousand long.

Who are the wild and crazy roadrunners who flock to this event? The veterans are Iowa residents who rally every year. Others are former residents who return to reclaim their roots. And year after year, more cyclists come from other states and other countries. They hear about this massive event and cannot pass up an opportunity to put their own foot to the pedal.

RAGBRAI is not a marathon. It's a love-athon.

"In all the years I've been coming from Washington [state] to Iowa for RAGBRAI, I have never heard a negative word," said Bill, a researcher for Weyerhaeuser. "There's nothing else like it in this country. It's where brain surgeons and truck drivers all bike together. It's the best," he said.

In the evening, bikers pile into town, hungry and tired and looking for a place to park their packs. Rows of food vendors are ready when the famished mob arrives. That's where we met a couple from Marysville, Missouri. Walking toward the city park and the shindig, a tall, lean young man gave us the details of his day—all superlatives. Endorphins still high, he even walked fast.

"Are you riders?" he asked. Bruce said, "Yes, with a 'W' (meaning writers)." I don't think our questioner got the joke. He just kept on talking.

After devouring a Meskwaki fry-bread taco, we focused on finding someone from our hometown, Cleveland, Ohio. We scanned the crowd for a clue. Before long we spied a woman wearing a familiar Emerald Necklace T-shirt. She had come all the way from Cleveland Heights to ride in RAGBRAI in honor of her upcoming fiftieth birthday. To chat with someone from back home gave us a great feeling.

We also met a participant from the Iowa Sesquicentennial bike tour across America. A group of three hundred people left Long Beach, California, on Memorial Day, destined to complete their journey in Washington D.C. on

Labor Day. They joined RAGBRAI for the week-long stretch across Iowa.

"It was a lifelong dream for me to take this trip," said Ed Steinbrech, a city government worker. "People envy my decision to risk losing my job. But if you're a biker, this is your only real dream."

What are bikers' real dreams? For some, it's the freedom of the open road, so open in Iowa you can see the crickets jump into the tall grass, and the dusty-blue cornflowers bow to the breeze along country roads. It's to listen to water trickling in the creeks and to hear the crying of the hawk and the red-winged blackbird and to smell the Iowa pigs and new-mown grass. It's to glide past cows in the pasture, to notice the lay of the land, and to wonder who might live in the farmhouses along dusty country roads.

It's to feel each bump and yield to every curve, for the dream follows nature's lead.

RAGBRAI is what Iowa is all about. When you ask an Iowan where he or she is from, the answer is, "south central Iowa," or "northeastern Iowa." I have never heard an Iowan use a town reference.

RAGBRAI is a unifying factor, this year a celebration of twenty-three years of statewide, community-to-community working-togetherness. RAGBRAI is like a grand family reunion, one we'll never forget.

Quaintly Connected

"Just talk to people and you will discover how connected we all are," said Elizabeth Costa of Downieville, California. The eighty-five-year-old who has survived cancer twice wasn't talking about smalltown gossip. She was referring to something far greater.

Elizabeth doesn't have to go far to validate her conviction that somehow we are all joined together. Like Girl Scouts selling cookies, the world knocks at her door.

Maybe that's because her house, a wood-framed, gingerbread-trimmed cottage built in 1857, is so inviting, and her yard is an enchanting assembly of fruit trees and flowering perennials. Spring, summer, and fall you can find Elizabeth plucking and pruning in her garden. The only thing that changes is her sunbonnet.

"One day a couple was walking by my front gate. They stopped to tell me how much they liked my flowers," she began. After a few minutes of conversation, Elizabeth ascertained that the duo was from Woodside, California.

"Oh, my college chum is from Woodside," she told them.

Elizabeth noticed the woman had a crippled leg, perhaps from polio. But it wasn't until she said that she owned a children's bookstore that a bell went off in Elizabeth's head. As if slamming her hand on a talk-show buzzer, she blurted out, "I've been swimming in your swimming pool when you weren't home."

The woman cracked a weird smile. Quickly, Elizabeth tossed out the missing link. "My college friend's name is Irene. When Irene injured her leg in an auto accident, she made arrangements with her friend, a bookstore owner, to use her swimming pool for rehabilitation. That must be you!" Elizabeth said.

The woman on the other side of the fence was smiling now. Moments later, they were all having tea together.

Costa has other stories.

"I've known Vance Lee since I was ten years old. That's seventy-five years," she said, lowering her head to peer over the top of her glasses. "We grew up together in Oakland, California. Our mothers were close friends. Vance and I both went to UC Berkeley. We were like family."

Vance married Katherine, and they had their first child. Then tragedy struck. The child, a son, died when he was just two years old.

"It was so strange," Elizabeth told. "The autopsy showed he had a needle in his heart. He must have been crawling around and somehow it got into his system."

In their grief, the Lees came to visit Elizabeth in the Sierra Mountains.

"Vance was a school principal in San Jose," Elizabeth continued. "His wife taught grammar school and was the organist at a big church. Eventually, they had two daughters. That was very nice, until tragedy struck again. One of the daughters, a music student at Cal Poly, was working for the summer as a camp counselor and was killed by a drunken driver."

Again, as a part of their healing process, the Lees visited Elizabeth. While they were expressing their sorrow, they also shared something they were doing to ease the pain. The Lees had established a scholarship award for the girl studying music at Cal Poly who "gave the most pleasure to people with her music," as their daughter had.

Elizabeth's grandson, Bob Fairchild, who also was visiting, mentioned that he happened to be a student at Cal Poly.

"Are you interested in music?" Vance asked.

"No," Bob said. "But my girlfriend Cheryl just received an award."

Within moments they all made the connection. Out of thousands of students, Cheryl had been chosen to receive the award from the Lees on behalf of their daughter.

"We were laughing and crying at the same time," Elizabeth said. "I guess the award gave us the most pleasure. We were dumbfounded to think that out of all the pain and agony, this gesture had come full circle back to us." Removing her glasses and wiping her eyes, she added, "If you are living life fully and openly, these things happen. If you shut yourself away, nothing ever happens."

10

It's Never Too Late

Truly believing in the power of goodness means it's never too late to correct an oversight, to mend hard feelings, to say "I love you," and to show real care. Most incredibly, it's never too late to forgive.

Crafting Iron Crosses

In north central South Dakota, trees are sparse, except for a few snags that survive the winter wind by rooting in gullies where they hide. And the town names tell the story of what it took to keep body and soul together on the prairie in the early 1900s: Faith, Hope, Chance, and Promise.

In the town of Timber Lake, one can easily imagine a cowhand coming out of KJ's Cafe or the sheriff strutting down Main Street with six-shooters hanging from his hips. That's where we met Kathy and Jim Nelson, seventeen-year residents and owners of the *Timber Lake Topic*, a weekly newspaper with a circulation of 1,500, more than twice the town's population! How could this be?

Most of the original Timber Lake homesteaders were German-Russian immigrants. Although many of their children have moved to the city, they still subscribe to the town's newspaper, and they return each year to the town celebration: The Days of 1910.

But not all of the second generation has moved away. One man in particular, Herman Kraft, has become a guardian of the past. He lives a few miles north and east of Timber Lake off Highway 20. A retired postal carrier and farmer, Herman hand tools handsome Damascus knives. One of his beauties is artfully placed in a circle on the mailbox that marks the entrance to the Kraft farm.

Herman Kraft, who taught himself the art of pounding steel, also learned to make Old World iron crosses because he saw a need.

"Once a friend told me that one of our high school classmates didn't have a marker on his grave, and he thought we should find a stone and make one," said Herman. "I said I would make him an iron cross, a tradition primarily used by Catholic German-Russian immigrants."

Herman Kraft, guardian of the past, handcrafts German-Russian crosses for unmarked graves in Glencross, South Dakota.

Then the story got bigger. Herman began noticing a number of unmarked graves in the Glencross Cemetery, near the town where he was raised. Fifteen graves of babies who died during the flu epidemic of 1918 had no markers. In the last seven years, Herman, who is one of sixteen children, handcrafted iron crosses for all those children he never knew.

Darkness Before Dawn

"We were devastated when we learned the tumor in Mom's pancreas was cancer," my cousin Paula wrote.

It was hard to believe that my mother's younger sister, Aunt Rosie, feisty, fit, and fearless Rosie, a young seventy-one, was dying.

As I sat motionless, staring at the letter, tears filled my eyes. I remembered my first experience with death. I recall coming through the back door after school in 1955—looking for oatmeal cookies and finding my mother in the kitchen ironing as if she were punishing the clothes, pressing the iron down so hard that I feared she'd smash the ironing board right to the ground. She was smoking a cigarette, something I never saw her do before. When she saw me, her skinny second grader, she burst into tears, which was foreign to me. Then she spilled the pain. Her mother, a woman she adored, had died, and she didn't even get to say goodbye to her. An Ellis Island immigrant who never learned English, her mother raised eight children with her husband to whom she was betrothed at birth.

Though my mother felt lost, she didn't let it extend into our lives. By suppertime, she was stirring the spaghetti sauce and reminding us to clean our rooms or there would be no watching *The Wonderful World of Disney* Sunday night.

That was some forty years ago. Now my cousin was reminding me what nobody wants to think about—that someday our parents will die.

I continued to read the letter. "When I learned that the tumor in Mom's pancreas was inoperable, I felt like someone kicked us in the gut, ripped our hearts out, and stomped on them," wrote Paula, the oldest daughter of Rosie's six children. "But Mom's illness brought us together as a family," she added. "We all had areas in our lives that needed healing, and the healing process had begun."

Rosie was a strong-willed, independent woman with reddish-brown hair. She didn't ask her children to help her cope with their father's alcoholism, something she often denied was "that bad." Ambivalence, however, is costly.

In the early 1970s, before we knew that alcoholism is a disease that affects the whole family, Paula, a young teen then, struggled to understand the confusion in her family. Over time, she carried the burden, developing anorexia nervosa, an emotional illness characterized by extreme weight loss that eats away at one's self-image.

"It was no coincidence that I was given the chance to complete what I had begun in psychotherapy as a teenager," Paula said. "I was able to tell Mom about my insights as an adult: that I finally realized that the anorexia was not my fault. I also forgave her for being overwhelmed and not knowing how to help me as a child. And I asked her to forgive me for not understanding all that she was dealing with."

"I think it helped to ease her transition. It surely allowed me to let her go, but that wasn't easy because we had grown so close in those last six weeks," Paula went on.

From the hospital Rosie was taken to Heather Knoll Nursing Home. "We could see that she wasn't getting stronger," Paula wrote. "One evening I saw the most beautiful sunset, and I knew Mom was going beyond that magnificent horizon to a place full of love and peace, a place I couldn't even begin to see or imagine."

The greatest gift during Rosie's illness was that, in her dying, she finally allowed her children to care for her. Rosie liked clean teeth, so Carol brushed and flossed them with a passion. Steve spent fifteen nights on the hospital floor on an air mattress so that he could be near his mom. She felt safer with someone there. Eric and his wife Holly arranged for their infant to be baptized in Rosie's hospital room. The child's name is Carmen, after Rosie's mom.

Nick really stuck his neck out. During the last week of her life, Rosie would eat only orange Popsicles. Nick went to Acme, opened three boxes of twenty-four assorted Popsicles, stuffed twenty-four orange ones in a box, closed it up, and made his purchase, adding some humor to a very difficult time. Paula's gift was sharing with her mother the deep personal feelings held in her heart. She promised that she would continue the healing process with the family. And in the end Amy and her husband Paul converted their spare bedroom into a sanctuary where the whole family could be with their mother.

"We had little over three precious hours with her," Paula said. "Everyone was there who needed to be there, and said what they needed to say. My hand was over Mom's heart. I felt the last beat of love she had to give in this life. There were tears trickling down her cheeks. She hadn't been able to cry before."

Before Rosie took her last breath, she tried to say something to Paul, her husband who has been sober for twenty-five years.

"I think she was trying to say that she loved him," Paula said. "Then she passed from this life into the next."

When Paula stepped outside her sister's house to walk home, she silently asked for a sign that her mother was okay. It had been a rainy day. For an instant the clouds parted and the sky opened. There was a brilliant white light and the sun passed through, round and full. It was as if heaven opened to receive her mother. Now she was perfect. Now she was whole.

Paula delivered a powerful message of hope at her mother's funeral. She acknowledged her brothers for coming great distances to be together. She spoke of love and forgiveness in the family. "We weren't perfect, and neither was Mom." And she thanked God for his hand in the healing process.

"It was a chance to share a very real part of me, perhaps one my family and relatives had never seen. I never realized so many people would be touched by it," she wrote. "It's amazing what happens when you let what you feel on the inside come out in the open."

Love's Bed of Roses

Bruce and I were first-time visitors at the Unitarian Universalist Church in Lakeland, Florida. When the minister invited newcomers to introduce themselves, we seized the opportunity to talk about our journey of hope.

After the service, a gracious woman with silver-gray hair approached us, extended her hand warmly, and began telling us about the tragic death of her two sons just eight weeks before.

I noticed people around us seemed oblivious to her pain, as if she were behind a screen. I glanced at Bruce. Without words we concurred, "What's wrong with this picture?"

We asked her if we could meet with her at a quieter place, perhaps at her home.

Three days later, we sat in the sun-filled living room of Etta and Harry Lawrence, listening. Though filled with grief, the woman, who was in her seventies, told a variety of amusing stories reminiscent of better days—about her boys' grade school years, how her son Terry was obsessed with airplanes since he was fourteen, and how he and his brother Lynn were good friends. She paused momentarily to show us their most recent pictures.

Then the nightmare.

What was supposed to be a day of picnicking and family fun shattered in tragic loss. Harry and his grandsons went up in the open-air bi-plane. Everything seemed fine. Then Terry and Lynn decided to take the Starduster II for one more spin.

"Just the two of them," their mother said.

Goggles tight across smiling faces, they climbed into the open cockpit and waved. Terry was a top-notch pilot. Both men had been majors in the Civil Air Patrol, and both had served on various search-and-rescue teams over the years. But this time there were no survivors. Terry, fifty-four, and Lynn, fifty-six, died instantly when, for no apparent reason, the plane plummeted to the ground.

Not only did Etta lose her sons, but most of her friends seemed to disappear that day, too.

"People don't know what to say to me. One person said, 'Be happy you had them for fifty-six years.' Yuck! Yet, I do appreciate it when they acknowledge my loss," she said, emphasizing the importance of caring words.

Then, placing her hand over her heart, she began telling a story about Terry's difficulty in verbalizing his love.

"Terry and I had a little game going. He knew I wanted him to say that he loved me, but he just wouldn't," Etta said. "He would buy me nice gifts, but he wouldn't say those three little words."

Mother and son spoke frequently long distance from Michigan to Florida. Etta always made a point of signing off with an "I love you." Terry would say, "Okay, mom. So long." Then he would laugh mischievously. Then click, he'd be gone.

One time Etta forgot the ritual and was about to say goodbye when Terry reminded her, "You forgot something Mom."

"Oh, yes," she said. "I love you."

A few nights before our talk, she had a dream. "I was half awake, half dozing when I saw a circle of diffused light, six feet in diameter," she said.

Front and center in the light stood Terry wearing a dark business suit. He leaned slightly forward and reached his hand downward, gesturing to a three-foot circle of roses in brilliant technicolor, velvety yellow, soft pink, snowy white, and ruby red.

"My mind was asking, what is he trying to tell me?" Etta said.

"Now is this proof enough?" was his answer.

In the dream, Lynn, who always expressed his affection openly with his mother, was sitting on a rock, knees pulled up with his arms, reflecting.

"She always knew that we loved her," he said to his brother.

Then the circle of light, the magnificent roses, and her sons were gone. Etta woke up.

"Before the dream, I thought that I just couldn't cry another tear, but I couldn't let go either. I felt a wonderful peace come over me after the dream. I knew my boys were together and they were all right," she said. "Then it occurred to me: Terry was saying he loved me."

Hope Springs Eternal

We sat captivated at Steve and Beth Parsons' kitchen table in Kansas. Each sentence echoed like a stone hitting the bottom of a dry but not forgotten well. Beth kept pouring us more tea, and Steve kept spilling more story.

Steve's mother was institutionalized for mental illness when he was just eighteen months old. He remembers riding on the bus with his older sister to see her. He also recalls being told by his father and stepmother that if he wasn't good, he would be sent to see his mother—as if that would be a kind of punishment.

Steve never saw it that way.

After his mother died in 1985, Steve became curious. Why wasn't his mother's family at the funeral? Had his mother's siblings—Julius, Ernie, and Sarah—vanished? Steve's mother had told his sister a tragic story about her family, the Fulks. Could it be true?

In January 1988, Steve and Beth started an eight-year search, beginning with a letter to the county where Steve's mother was born. Nothing was found.

That March, Beth, a genealogy enthusiast, gave Steve an album of old family photos, an anniversary gift that chronicled his father's side of the family. But the real gift was two color slides of his mother from 1948.

"They were beautiful," Beth said. "Steve's father had kept them in a lockbox for forty years."

In June 1989, Beth drove to Florida and uncovered Steve's mother's birth certificate in a "delayed records" file. She found no account of any family tragedy.

Not satisfied, in 1990 the couple dug deeper, one county over. Amazingly, they found information that led to meeting a distant cousin who lived close by—just a half hour from their rural Kansas home.

"At the kitchen table, Cousin Hazel pulled a frayed, yellowed newspaper clipping from her wallet and said sadly that she couldn't keep the truth from us," Beth said.

Steve read in silence the 1959 shocking headline and article about how his Uncle Ernie, who had left the farm to become a horse groomer at a New Jersey racetrack, hanged himself. Three days later, his Aunt Sarah, the youngest of three surviving Fulk children, shot their father on their farm in northern Florida. Then Sarah walked two miles to the main road, caught a ride into town, and turned herself in. Within a few days, Sarah was transferred to a state mental hospital. There was never a trial.

Steve hedged. "Did I really want to pursue such a tragedy?" he asked himself. "This could be as mean as snakes." But something inside of him pressed on.

"I just couldn't give up the hope that there might be one person left in the world that looks like my mother," he said.

In July 1991, Steve and Beth returned to Florida to continue the search. In the dingy basement of a county courthouse, they found a dust-covered "insanity docket." Inside was the notation "nol-pros" beside Sarah Fulk's name. Though Aunt Sarah would never be emotionally able to stand trial, somehow she did manage to disappear in 1970. She was thirty-seven. There was no record of her discharge.

Steve and Beth hired a genealogist in Florida hoping to find Aunt Sarah and Uncle Julius.

Beth, who is a mental health nurse, suspects that Sarah had a psychotic break in 1959. Sarah's whole world had fallen apart. Her mother died four years earlier. Her sister (Steve's mother) was lost to mental illness. Brother Julius was in California, and now Ernie was dead. Sarah was like a captive. Her father was so protective of her. She could not leave his sight. Sarah's dream had been that Ernie would come back to the farm and rescue her.

Steve learned that Sarah had perceived her father as having laughed at Ernie's funeral (an odd yet not uncommon response for those who have difficulty expressing emotions). The following day, Sarah, taking great offense to this behavior, took a .22 squirrel rifle that was under the kitchen sink and shot her father in the back of the head while he was eating lunch. When Sarah thought there was no hope, her mind snapped.

But where was she now?

The land held the secret. In August 1995, folks whom Steve and Beth had never met came forward with help and astonishing news. The Fulk farmland had never been settled, and on the land deed Steve's mother was listed as the lost heir. If Steve and his siblings didn't come forward by January 1998, the land in its entirety would go to Uncle Julius' only child, Adam Fulk of Arkansas. Sadly, Julius had died in 1974, but the land deed had his son's address on it.

Using the phone book on CD-ROM, Steve located Adam by phone on the first try. "It was wonderful," Beth said. "Adam was able to give us Aunt Sarah's address."

Beth recalls praying, "Oh, God, prepare their hearts." Then she got an inner message: "It's already done." Steve telephoned his mother's only living sibling. Aunt Sarah knew who he was and remembered Steve's brother and sister. She invited Steve to write to her. The reconnection had begun.

A month later Steve and Beth walked the Fulk land for the first time. "There is a crystal-clear spring on the property, and the long pine forest had dropped a carpet of soft brown needles. It was as quiet as a sanctuary," Beth told us.

Still, Steve worried. "Was it right to interrupt the land?" Beth encouraged him. "There is multigenerational healing to be done here," she said.

The next day they met Aunt Sarah. There was such a gentleness about her, and she was able to tell them some of her story. After Sarah left the hospital in 1970, she married James, a kind man. They had two children, Marie and Bill (named after Sarah's father). After a few years, Sarah was rehospitalized.

"When I get to know you better, I'll introduce you to my children," Sarah told them.

Then she asked Steve if he liked the farm. "Yes, it's a beautiful and peaceful place," he said.

"After I was released from the state hospital, I went back to the farm and walked all over it," Sarah said. "Then I left. I don't need to go back. It's okay if you like it, Steve."

Steve continued to build his relationship with his Aunt Sarah, and in July 1996, he began to get letters and e-mail from Marie and Bill. "They sounded like me," Steve told us. "Could I have something in common with first cousins I had never met?"

A few months later, Aunt Sarah invited Steve and Beth to visit and meet her children, Marie and Bill, and their father James. They shared photo albums, stories, and laughter for the first time. The visit stretched to eight hours as they made plans for the future. A bonding had begun.

The intention to heal is a powerful force. On April 26, 1997, on the Fulk family farm, Steve and Beth, along with family and friends, held a "Blessing Ceremony"—a kind of rite of passage to release the past symbolically and move the Fulk family into the future, reunited.

Steve and Beth's search for Steve's family roots continues to be a growth experience for everyone. Steve found his family and himself. "I never knew where my determination to see things through, persistence to make things right, and that real soft spot in me came from," he said. "It was my mother's side of the family."

One Shining Moment

Lynne Mouw, former publisher of the St. Ansgar, Iowa *Enterprise Journal*, was cleaning out the back room of her office, tossing out old files and stacks of yesterday's news. She wasn't alone. Two salvage guys were lugging an old typesetting machine out to their big truck, and a thin unkempt dog was on the sidelines, peering through the open door. What etiquette. The canine didn't even come in.

Lynne asked the men if the dog was with them. The men said it wasn't their dog. Lynne, a dog lover, moved closer and began to communicate with the Airedale.

"Tucker?" she asked, squinting her eyes and tilting her head. Could this shabby creature be the pet of her friends, Jay and Ruby Black of Clear Lake? "Tucker, what are you doing here?"

The Blacks, who have a spunky Airedale, had stopped by the Mouws on their way through town a few days ago. Maybe Tucker had gotten away. Maybe he was lost.

Lynne opened the screen door and invited the floppy-eared animal inside. The gentle pet followed her into her office and sat patiently beside Lynne while she called the thought-to-be owners.

"It can't be Tucker," said Jay, on the other end of the line. "Tucker is sitting right here next to me. We're sharing a bowl of popcorn. Tell me more about this lost dog."

Lynne said it was the nicest, most gentle dog she had ever met. But what was she to do? The friends chatted a little longer, then decided that Lynne would call the dog pound and the police department to see if anyone had lost an Airedale. Then she would call Jay back.

Indeed, there had been several calls about this "female, lost Airedale with wiry-gray hair." The angelic animal had been roaming around town for several days. She wasn't bothering anybody, but some were bothered that she wasn't cared for. No one claimed her.

Lynne was advised to let her out. Maybe she would go home, wherever that was.

Lynne opened the front door, and the dutiful dog sauntered outside.

"Something kept tugging at my heart. It didn't seem right," said Lynne, "But I didn't know what to do with this poor, lost, homeless creature."

Lynne called Jay. "When I said I had let her go, you'd have thought the world was coming to an end!" said Lynne.

"Go and find her and call me right back when you have her in your possession! I love Airedales and don't want her to go through anymore hardship," Jay said. "I'll come get her and give her a good home."

So off Lynne went, driving around in the rain looking for the nicest and about-to-be-luckiest dog in the world.

"As I drove around town, I thought of all the good hiding places and began to worry that I wouldn't be able to find her. Not only had I lost the dog, but also I was sure to lose our friends if I didn't find her!" she said.

Lynne finally spotted the dog. She wasn't hiding. She was lying on the wet grass out in the open, chewing on a bone she had scavenged. Anxious that the pet would try to escape, Lynne slowly approached her and gingerly slipped a makeshift collar over her dripping wet head. Gently, she encouraged the lost soul to walk with her.

She came along happily as if Lynne had passed a test, not she!

Back in her office Lynne made a blanket bed, filled a water bowl, and offered the nameless dog some food. Then she called the soon-to-be owners.

"She's here. She's comfortable, and I'm heading to the store to get her some Kibbles and Bits," she told Jay.

"Great! I'm on my way. What do you think we should name her?" he asked.

Lynne told him he probably needed to meet her before naming her. "I'm on my way," he said.

The homeless dog and the happy new owner became instant friends. All seemed well until Jay stroked her matted coat, and she shyly let him know of a very tender spot on her right flank. Maybe she had been hit by a car or injured in some way. Jay would take her to the vet in the morning after a good bath and gentle grooming.

The rescuers decided to name the lost pet, Shanta, from a favorite passage in Robert James Waller's essay, "Southern Flight." "It seemed to fit her," said Lynne.

Jay lifted Shanta carefully placing her on a blanket in the back of his covered pickup. He promised to let Lynne know what the vet said after their visit.

"I felt good about it," Lynne said.

However, the next day's news wasn't so good. After examining Shanta, the vet determined that she had a chronic degenerative bone disease and was in constant pain with no hope of getting better. He estimated her age at about ten years and commented about what a nice dog she was. But he recommended that she be put down to rescue her from her pain.

"It was a tough call," said Lynne. "At least her last twenty-four hours on earth were filled with warmth and caring. She came into our lives for but a brief shining moment and touched our hearts."

11

Listening to the Voice

What does it mean to listen to an inner voice? Too often the mind chatters away and the heart gets second billing. Once the **shoulds** and **shouldn'ts** are sorted through, then comes the challenge of quieting the mind long enough to hear the still, small voice within. The message may come through a dream. It may be crystal clear or as subtle as a passing thought, one that lingers—asking to be turned over like a pretty rock. Beware! As in the wink of an eye, the voice can jump right out of your mouth with wisdom that will astound you. You'll think, "Who said that?"

It was **the voice.**

The Field of Dreams

W. P. Kinsella, author of *Field of Dreams*, wrote with the spirit of America on the tip of his pen. He knew what brings people to baseball fields.

Universal Studios knew his story would bring people to movie theaters, but no one ever dreamed it would bring people from around the globe to a cornfield in Dyersville, Iowa.

Our first visit to The Field was on a late Thursday afternoon. Even our red pickup was eager to get there, kicking up a rooster tail of dust as we followed the signs toward the movie site three miles out of town.

The sun was beginning its descent, illuminating the corn, making the silky greens seem greener and the long shadows of late afternoon seem deeper and more receptive to the unknown.

A handful of dreamers sat in the stands. A few picture-takers walked in and out of the tall green corn. We sat in the bleachers and soaked up the warm evening sun. A thick, velvet-like quiet wrapped us in a moment of endless time.

Spontaneously, I leaned forward and began talking to a woman from Bloomington, Illinois. She said she loved the movie *Field of Dreams* because it didn't need sex and violence to make it great. I nodded. A part of me wanted to confess that I had seen the movie a dozen times. It changed my life. After all, wasn't this journey across America our Field of Dreams? But the magic of Iowa and the memory of all I learned about following your heart told me to keep silent.

Then a man leaned forward and said, "Right after I saw the movie, a deer poked his nose out of our cornfield and walked onto our lawn. It never happened before, and it hasn't happened since."

We all nodded. I noticed their eyes were glowing with aliveness.

Baseball is a vital part of the American culture. Thus, two neighbors work together to make The Field available to the public, free of charge. Al and Rita Ameskamp own left field, and Don Lansing owns the remaining field, plus the white farmhouse with the wrap-around porch and inviting swing.

"In the beginning," Al said, "I didn't see much in the picture until producer Brian Frankish told me it's not really about baseball—it's about the love of the game."

On peak weekends in the summer, more than three thousand come to The Field. Maybe it's what brought us back on Sunday afternoon.

On this Sunday, people came to support the Iowa Special Olympics, to sit on the lawn with fellow travelers, and just to participate in a community event.

We met a father and son from Wisconsin. Zachary, sixteen months, has his own form of baseball. He loves running in and out of the corn while his dad, dressed in a Cleveland Indians' jersey and hat, plays along. It's a different kind of catch.

At high noon, sun pouring down on nearly a thousand spectators, the soundtrack from the movie draws our attention to The Field. The Ghost Players (many of the original movie cast dressed in vintage White Sox uniforms) emerge from left field, and the crowd howls. The umpire shouts, "Play ball!"

Then crack! It's a line drive to right field. The first baseman, a Ghost Player, playfully fumbles the return throw. Then, racing with a smile as wide as the state of Iowa, a youth jumps both feet onto first base and gives his partner, a member of the Confederate Railroad country music band, a hardy hand slap. The umpire calls it: "Safe." The crowd cheers, and the pitcher throws his hat in the dust.

As predicted in the movie, the people do come. Older folks come to savor memories of a time when America was younger and greener. The young come to bat a few balls and to boast that they "hit one" at the Field of Dreams. Vacationers come to touch the quiet of the midwestern lifestyle and to listen to *the voice*. And we came to savor a slice of America captured by an inspiring movie coupled with the love of a game. That it brings people from around the world together in one simple baseball field, once full of corn, is delightfully American.

Sweet Surrender

If remembering your favorite things—as in "bright-colored packages tied up with string"—from a popular Rogers and Hammerstein musical, dissolves sadness, what transforms despair?

We found an answer near California's great San Joaquin Valley in the former copper and silver mining town of Acton, just north of Los Angeles. While standing in line at the Acton Market, we met Ariel McCloud, a vibrant widow in her seventies who rides her horse every day!

Ariel had accidentally purchased a box of dates and was eager to return them. We invited her to go ahead of us in line—a simple act of kindness that stunned her.

"It just seems nobody does that anymore," she said. We smiled and gave her our Bounty Hunting card.

The next day Ariel called and invited us to join her at Don Cucos, her favorite Mexican restaurant. Two hours later, we were sitting on red leather seats in a cozy booth, enjoying spicy food and telling stories. We told about our decision to go on the road.

Ariel spoke about her family, her passion for horses, and the history of Acton, the town she loves.

What a delight to hear the story of how Ariel brought in eighty head of cattle and a bull on her honeymoon many years ago. Today, she still wears white boots and blue jeans that complement her elegant cowgirl appearance.

Ariel McCloud of Acton, California, rides her horse every day and has a passion for life.

But the most incredible story was the one about her husband Nick. Many years ago, Ariel and Nick were on a car trip. A mother's intuition told Ariel to move their three-year-old daughter from the front seat into the back—just in time. Suddenly, there was a terrible accident that left Ariel in a coma for thirty days.

The child was unharmed. Ariel was hospitalized in one facility, and Nick was hospitalized in another, a VA hospital. Nick was deeply worried about his wife. He prayed and prayed for her recovery. He was beginning to give up.

"In his deepest hour of despair, he completely turned my well-being over to God," said Ariel. "As soon as he released it, Nick fell asleep, and in a dream he saw Jesus sitting calmly on a rock. He got the message: Everything was going to be fine."

Nick woke up with renewed hope. Without hesitation, he checked himself out of the VA hospital and headed straight for his wife's bedside. There he found Ariel with her eyes open. She was just waking up.

Little Brother Is Big Hero

Jennifer Palmer is just a year older than her big-hearted little brother. While we were in New Mexico, she called us from her home in Louisiana. "When I read about you two traveling around gathering stories of unsung heroes, I thought, 'This is my opportunity to honor my brother.'"
Last winter, Jennifer was visiting her parents, Wanda and Bill Kimmel in Lafayette, Ohio, and her brother John from Grove City, near Columbus.

"John and I were leaving our parents' house. Before leaving, John said, 'Let me hug Mom just one more time.' We were on our way to a meeting when I heard my brother say that we were going to have an accident," Jennifer said.

Sliding toward them was a semi-truck hauling huge rolls of steel. A thought flashed through Jennifer's mind: "Was this why John said an extra goodbye to Mom?"

John pressed the brakes just in time. The truck skidded by. The heavy cargo was thrown off, leaving huge holes in the ground. The truck cab landed on its side off the road, and John and Jennifer were not harmed. But the driver of the truck was trapped in the cab, seriously injured.

Jennifer ran to the nearest farmhouse for help. When she returned a few minutes later, several people had gathered around the smoking rig.

"They were standing there, doing nothing," she recalls.

Then, as if something came alive in her brother, John moved through the crowd. The truck driver, afraid the rig was going to blow up, was waving everyone to back off. Everyone did, except John. He seemed tuned in to something else. "He put his foot through the windshield of the cab and lifted the guy right out, with no hesitation," Jennifer said, as if to say, "Wow! That's my brother!"

The state patrol and ambulance arrived moments later. "The whole thing happened in less than fifteen minutes," Jennifer said.

Why was John able to act when others were not? Jennifer recalls what was so amazing. "John simply disregarded the external directions," she said.

When the brother and sister team were back in their car, Jennifer turned to her brother and said, "John, do you realize what you did?"

Like most ordinary heroes, her brother said, "No."

John and Jennifer's story gives us the opportunity to tout another hero from Ohio— one who just happens to be one of our sons.

In October 1996, Lance Corporal Jesse Madsen, twenty-two, was assigned to watch the gear of participants running in the annual Marine Corps Marathon. He fell asleep for a short while, and, by chance, became the humorous subject for a *Quantico Sentry* staff photographer.

When Jesse woke up, he began walking around to shake off the nap. After all, he started working at 4:00 A.M. Later that morning, Jesse spotted a woman about fifty yards away who appeared to be in distress.

"She seemed to be calling for help but not out loud," he said.

*Lance Corporal
Jesse Madsen,
Cleveland, Ohio*

Madsen changed his pace and began running toward her. When he was just five feet away, she collapsed in his arms.

Jesse called the staff sergeant to ask him to get help. When he got no response, he called for the MP (military police) standing nearby.

"I thought he could get a medic, but he was so hesitant that I just picked her up and ran her over to the medical tent myself," he said.

The woman was still unconscious when the med-vac helicopter flew her off to the hospital. The medical team in the tent told Jesse he probably saved her life.

Ironically, Jesse was in the newspaper because he was caught napping! The caption said, *J. P. Madsen takes a break from gear watch.* It should have said, *Lance Corporal Madsen rests before rescuing damsel in distress.*

We probably all have something noble inside of us just waiting to get out. These two heroes from Ohio are proof.

Picketing Power Turns Bad Guys Out

When a ninety-two-year-old woman asked her family to take her to Mesquite, Nevada, to celebrate her birthday by joining a picket line against pornography, her family brought her to the desert border town, cake and all. And when they asked her why, she proudly announced, "I want one more opportunity to stand up for the Lord."

The assistants at the Nevada Visitors' Center are still talking about the little town that made national news last year. We wanted to hear more, so we interviewed Dena Hoff, president of H.O.M.E. (Help Our Moral Environment), a nonprofit organization launched in 1993 to educate the public about the dangers of pornography.

"Mesquite is anything but a sleepy little border town," Dena said. "I think the owner of the pornography store thought we were helpless. He was wrong."

When the Mesquite Chamber of Commerce learned of the threat to their small town, they quickly organized a program featuring a video that spelled out the adverse secondary effects of pornographic establishments: increased vandalism and burglary, associated drug use, increased prostitution, and crimes of sexual violence.

Five years ago, Dena, her husband, and their two daughters moved to Mesquite from Las Vegas, hoping to escape such negative influences.

"When I walked out of that video, I was convinced that pornography must be stopped," said Dena. "It was a moral issue."

Then an inner voice clinched a partnership.

"It was as if God said, 'You do your part. I'll do mine, and it will all work out,'" said Dena.

Her part was to become knowledgeable and to get involved. That's how H.O.M.E. was started when six core citizens came together to design a city-wide plan of action. They would educate the public, write letters to their legislators, and set up a twenty-four-hour-a-day, seven-day-a-week picket line. Ultimately, they would take whatever legal action they could to shut down the hard-core pornography store.

And what was God's part?

In all the time that volunteers were traveling, sometimes in eighty-mile-an-hour winds, no one was hurt. During a seventeen-day hot spell in June 1996, when temperatures rose to 117 degrees, they had a shelter. The Virgin River Casino allowed the group to construct a small house next to the porn shop.

"Right from the start we felt protected," she said.

Dena says that the most difficult part was facing the ugly facts about pornography in the United States. According to statistics released by H.O.M.E., adolescent boys are among the largest consumers of hard-core pornography. At least one woman over age eighteen is raped every forty-six seconds, and pornography serves as the instruction manual.

"You can't fight something like this without a belief in a loving God," she said. "Otherwise, you would become too despairing or cynical."

The easier part was setting up and maintaining the picket line. As soon as the word about Mesquite's plight hit the press, carloads of concerned citizens from neighboring communities—southern Utah, Arizona, and Nevada—arrived, eager to exercise their First Amendment rights.

The group formed the longest, continuously running, nonunion picket line in history. They marched for thirty long months with homemade signs:

PORN HURTS KIDS
WE WILL NEVER GIVE UP
ONE YEAR—WE'RE STILL HERE
PORN IS POLLUTION.

"We took a stand, upholding community and family values," said Dena.

The picketing effort alone required 88,000 man hours, that's forty-four years of work at an eight-hour job. And eight thousand volunteers answered the call, traveling one and three-quarter million miles. That's seven and three-tenths one-way trips to the moon.

After the first year of picketing, the pornography store owner threatened the six core members with a lawsuit. He said that if they stopped picketing, he'd drop the charges. After extensive depositions by picketers' attorneys and nothing by the porn store owner, the suit was dismissed.

But on March 15, 1996, the casino asked for the land back, giving the picket line until April 1 to vacate the property. This meant giving up their only shelter. Despite weakened support, Dena and the crew held strong.

"I knew it would all work out," she said. "I just didn't know how."

On March 28 the Federal court upheld Mesquite's city ordinance in its entirety, forcing the porn shop to close.

"The porn store owner was trying to make this into a Constitutional issue," said Dena. "He lost."

Some volunteers are melancholy that the time of banding together is over. They liked the opportunity to be accountable Americans, making a difference.

Dena Hoff has become a national speaker for the ending of pornography. And the group continues to serve by distributing valuable information.

For a package of information on how to sustain a picket line against pornography, see H.O.M.E.'s web page: www.sisna.com/mesquite/home.

Bus Stops for Prayer

Stories about listening to the deep, still voice surfaced across America. In the western corner of South Carolina, we met Paula Heusinkveld, a professor of Spanish at Clemson University. After learning about our project, Paula volunteered to have a potluck dinner. She invited guests to bring a covered dish and a story. Her mother, who was visiting from Atlanta, Georgia, brought this one.

"Once when I was traveling, I met a man in a bus terminal," Emma Lou said, then paused and looked over her bifocals.

"I'm a person of quiet faith, and I always try to mind my own business. Well, the man asked me if I would join him for a midday drink. I was afraid that he had a drinking problem, and sure enough, he did."

On a weekend pass from a veterans' hospital, the anxious traveler was en route to visit a daughter he had not seen in two years. He needed emotional support.

"Truly, I didn't know how to help him," Emma Lou admitted. "I didn't know anything about alcoholism."

Then, out of the blue, the words came to her. "I told him that what I could do was to pray with him."

The man graciously accepted her offer. Together the two strangers quietly prayed on their knees in the noisy bus terminal. Those around them, many who had also been approached by the man, were in awe.

After they prayed, the man asked Emma Lou to dispose of the liquor bottle. She quickly placed it in her purse. Both travelers were relieved that it was out of sight. It was also out of mind and in the hands of someone who Emma Lou is convinced, "knows more about these matters than I do."

She said that telling the story makes her smile and helps her remember to let go and allow that deeper wisdom to surface more often.

12

Bravo

J ust before embarking on our journey across America, Bruce had a dream. In the dream he was leading a cheer. Over time, the dream became more clear: Everyone needs something to cheer about. Otherwise, we live in a world without hope. Too dangerous!

We had been complaining for eons about the demoralizing effect of the nightly news. It was time to do something about it—highlight what's positive.

The stories we gathered from the lives of children profoundly carried this message of hope. For innocence is to a child what grace is to an adult. It's just easier to see it in children.

Kids Veto Violence

In March 1995 twenty-three Thurston Elementary School second graders in Springfield, Oregon, tallied 649 incidents of TV violence in twelve hours of their favorite shows.

And when they confronted big business, saying *no* to violent TV programming and *no* to the sponsors who support it, the whole nation said *yes*.

The idea started when Susan Colonna told her class that the "program police" were going to put a black box on their TV to monitor the programs they watch.

"That got their attention," she said. Then she confessed that she wasn't telling the truth. They could learn to monitor programs themselves by identifying what is violent behavior. The children brainstormed six categories for the survey: kicking, threats, hitting, weapons, bombs, and other.

"The kids were amazed at how many times they were viewing violence and not knowing it," their teacher said.

Next, students wrote letters to advertisers saying they were boycotting their products and their shows, including the popular Power Rangers.

Then they designed a Declaration of Independence from Violence, stating, "The world must have less violence so that children may live safe and happy lives."

Their efforts didn't stop there. They wrote to members

of Congress, U.S. Senators, fellow second-graders in Lane County and, of course, to the White House.

As interest grew, newspapers and TV stations covered the story. And when ABC's *World News Tonight* with Peter Jennings came to visit their school, the children knew they were truly making a difference. From coast to coast, cards and letters poured in like confetti at a hero's parade. Sympathetic viewers wrote to get the boycott list. Students and teachers from schools across America wrote to thank them and ask for a copy of the Declaration from Violence.

A year later, we stopped in to visit the kids. Eight students, now third-graders, came bounding into the back of their favorite teacher's classroom, smiling, giggling, and eager to meet us. Quickly, they assembled on the floor— their customary posture for sharing and storytelling.

Bruce introduced us as a traveling news team. Pointing out our journey from Ohio to Oregon on a large U.S. map, he said, "We are here to interview you because what you have done is worth cheering about." Then we asked what has changed for them since they started the project.

They said they are still boycotting violent shows.

"I ride my bike more," said a boy dressed in blue.

"My mother called the cable TV company and had them take off the channels that weren't good for us," said a girl with blonde curly hair.

"I don't watch those shows anymore, and neither does my little brother because he watches what I watch," said a youngster, as if proud to be influencing his family in a positive way.

Another child reported he still takes the boycott list to

the grocery store. And a girl in deep thought reflected on a time she and her brother went to Burger King with their grandmother. When her grandma allowed her brother to have a gargoyle toy he got in a Fun Meal, the girl said, "My mom does not allow those toys." And when the grandmother said it was OK, the enlightened student exclaimed, "Grandma, what are you saying?"

Bottom line: The students learned to make choices, to speak up, and to say no when violence darkens their way.

All too quickly the bell rang, and the students who made national news hurried off to their next class, all smiles.

Soon Colonna's present class of second-graders was filing in through Room 7's door, ready to meet two visitors from Ohio. Telling them briefly about our journey to gather good news in America, we held up an example: Fifteen hand-drawn pictures from Joyce Pope's first-grade class in Cleveland, Ohio, showing what made them smile.

Here is what they said: *Tom got his cast off and he smiled; Jasmine went to the beach on her birthday and she smiled; Shardey moved to a new house and she smiled; Alex was invited to play with Nate after school and he smiled; Stephanie went all the way across the big bars and she smiled!*

When Colonna's second-graders shared with us what makes them smile, we felt the strength of David having defeated Goliath.

"We underestimate what kids can do," said Colonna.

Teens Stand Up for the Trees

Nobody yells, "Timber!" anymore. They holler, "Uphill," which is precisely the direction the Pacific Northwest is facing regarding the logging industry. Will big-tree logging or the trees be preserved? Everybody has something to say about it, and nobody knows for sure.

Once, more than two million acres of redwood forest graced the California coastline—a forest so thick that early explorer Jedediah Smith had to cut a path to the Pacific. By 1965 there were 300,000 acres left as ancient forests fell into private ownership.

In a late effort to save the "big ones," Congress set aside Redwood National Park in 1968. Yet only two to five percent of the original, old-growth redwood forest is preserved in our national and state park systems. Today, forest activists wage another battle—one against clear cutting and the abrupt loss of trees more than two hundred years old. How will aggressive logging affect tomorrow's generations?

In Oregon we met a band of spunky teenage girls standing up for the Douglas fir, a stand of trees at nearby Warner's Creek. On a chilly October night, instead of cheering at a football game, fourteen freshmen and sophomores congregated on the steps of the Federal Building in downtown Eugene. This Friday night would be spent in nonviolent, "hot conversation" about the cold facts: They were on a hunger strike, protesting the latest bad news.

"Old laws that once protected the forest are no longer in effect," said an adult activist, standing on the steps. "Recently, like July 27, a 'rider' slid by Congress that allows salvage logging—something that could encourage willful burning of old forests."

Two teens, Anita and Ariel, discovered the forest activists while riding their bikes downtown. "We were lost and stopped to find out what their signs were about," Ariel said.

The two girls went back to their school and spread the word, enrolling others in the weekend camp-out and fast.

"We can't vote yet. There needs to be something for us to do to show our concern," Ariel said.

"We don't want to wait until we're out of college to make a difference," chimed in Molly.

Enlightened by teenagers who were making a difference, we began to listen for logging conversations. Everywhere we went, we heard people talking.

"We won the last round," said our waitress in Cave Junction, Oregon, referring to the loggers over the environmentalists. Her apron pulled tight, dark hair secured in a neat ponytail, the hardworking woman in her forties poured coffee, cleaned up crumbs, and sawed away at our naiveté. She was buzzing with the freewheeling spirit that brought tough men across the Rockies to clear land and build pioneer towns in the Wild West.

But then she softened, "There does need to be some kind of checks and balances on the system," she said.

While in Redwood National Park, we stopped to see The Big Tree. Not far off U.S. Route 101 stands a huge redwood with twelve-inch thick bark. Her base is twenty-two feet in diameter, and she reaches 360 feet heavenward. This 1,500-year-old tree is truly a survivor.

One more stop filled in the gaps. At the dark, smoky Lumberjack Bar in Orick, Oregon, we encountered a retired logger behind the counter. "What'll ya have?" asked the old man. After ordering a beer and a burrito, we munched on peanuts and started a conversation.

"I guess you've seen The Big Tree," I said, opening up a sore subject.

"You betcha'," he said with a Paul Bunyan laugh. "I'd like to fell that one."

"Really?" I said. This old-timer knows the good old days are over, but he'll never stop boasting about them.

"There was a time when logging was legal, and this town was so alive," he said, shaking his head.

The words "so alive" reminded us of our friends, the teenagers sleeping on cold cement. It was Saturday night. What was happening at the Federal Building? On our way back to our campsite, we stopped to find out.

"We are cold and hungry," said Molly, bundled in blankets, snuggling with nine classmates. "But we are learning to trust," she said with a smile.

"Remember, we are the generation raised not even to trust Halloween candy. We have accepted blankets and encouragement from absolute strangers!" she said.

What the teenagers may not know is that big-tree logging is a tough business. But after the hunger strike weekend, they know that preserving the forest is tough work, too.

Child's Determination Counts

There is much good news in America, and there are loads of people who want to share it. In one two-week period, we received nearly seventy phone calls from people suggesting stories for us. One such call, from Sue O'Neil in Mesa, Arizona, brought tears to our eyes.

Three years ago, when her son Kevin was eight, his Cub Scout troop went camping for the first time. The parents were invited to come along and sleep—not in tents like their sons, but in cozy cabins.

Kevin was an exuberant, outgoing child, but the morning after the camp-out, Kevin came to his mother, struggling to walk. She asked if he'd slept in clothes that were wet from the creek? He had not, he said.

"Just move around and warm yourself up," she suggested. The problem went away.

The next day Sue went to Kevin's Little League game. Kevin had always been a "macho kid," but when he limped off the field complaining that someone had pushed him, Sue looked to the coach for an explanation.

"No, Kevin was running, and he fell," the coach said.

Sue wrapped Kevin's ankle and sent him off to school the next day. But when the school nurse called and said Kevin had lost the use of one of his hands, Sue was alarmed.

She took her son directly to the doctor. While at the doctor's office, Kevin lost use of his other arm.

During a two-year struggle, Kevin kept losing the use of different limbs. Then he would regain function. For a while he was in a wheelchair. He missed a lot of school. As his body weakened, so did his self-esteem.

The doctors couldn't find the cause, so Sue and her husband took their son to the Mayo Clinic in Rochester, Minnesota. By that time his self-esteem was zero.

"At Mayo's the doctors said Kevin had fibromyalgia," Sue said. "We began whirlpool treatments, vitamin therapy, and muscle-building exercises."

However, nothing seemed to make a real difference. The strange symptoms persisted, so the desperate mom started her own search. At one point she insisted doctors treat Kevin for Lyme disease, which is caused by ticks. One month of powerful antibiotics stopped the problems, but only briefly.

Then the music teacher at Kevin's school told Sue about another student who was suffering from similar symptoms. Sue met the child's mother, a medical doctor. The doctor thought the children's illness must be an allergic reaction because the symptoms didn't resemble a disease process.

The mothers joined forces, checking laundry detergents, medicine cabinets, and anything they had in common. Just one clue surfaced: Both homes had carpets cleaned by the same company. Although this evidence was inconclusive, all carpet cleaning stopped.

Kevin was also tested for allergies and found to be allergic to peanuts. That may have been the culprit.

After two years, Kevin started back to school. "He was doing better, but he he'd lost confidence in his body," Sue said. "I prayed, *'Lord, please give my son his confidence back.'*"

Not long after that, Sue read in a magazine about an art contest for children, offering a big cash prize. Kevin was now eleven years old, and like most pre-teens, he was motivated by money. Sue approached him with the challenge: "Kevin, if you draw a picture that depicts harmony and peace in the world, you can win $25,000."

Sue admits she had to stretch herself to believe this was possible. Her logical mind knew this was a long shot, but her heart said, *'Encourage him to try.'*

Kevin went far beyond "try." Although he could hardly hold a pencil, he decided he was going to win the contest. With pointed determination, he drew the picture ten minutes at a time. Because he loves the piano, he drew the world and wrapped a huge keyboard around it. Then he made the children of the world playing together from wherever they lived.

Kevin didn't win the national contest, but he won the top prize for the state of Arizona from among six thousand participants—a hundred dollars worth of children's books.

"When he opened the letter, he was screaming for joy," Sue said.

"I knew I could do it," he said over and over.

Kevin's mother knew her prayers had been answered. Her son had regained his confidence. Incidentally, Kevin, now twelve, made the school basketball team this year.

Gymnasts Break the Barriers

As a young child, Deby Hergenrader wondered why she and her brother could take swimming lessons in Fresno, California, but her younger sister Kathy could not.

"The teacher said there was a special place for Kathy. But where was that special place?" Deby asked, squinting.

Not until junior high school, when one of Deby's friends used the word *retarded* were Deby's eyes opened. The friend quickly apologized, but "I realized the world did not know about Kathy," Deby said.

She began bringing her friends over to meet her special sister. "I would say, 'Do Ed Sullivan,' and Kathy would imitate Sunday night's TV hero. 'Do the splits,' I'd say, so she would demonstrate how flexible Down's Syndrome children are."

But in high school, Deby excelled in gymnastics, and Kathy remained on the sidelines.

"When I was competing, I didn't have much time for my sister," Deby said.

But the hand of fate soon redrew the lines. In 1972 Deby, an Olympic qualifier, injured her ankle. She would not be an Olympic star.

In time, however, she would become a champion of a different sort.

The next year, Deby met Steve Hergenrader, a member of the New York Yankees' farm team, who was volunteering with the Special Olympics. Deby watched Steve coach Kathy's softball team.

"I fell in love with him when I saw him with my sister," she said.

The couple married in 1975, started a family, and launched a dream—beginning with a backyard gymnastics class where able-bodied and disabled could learn together.

In the class a vision-impaired child was matched with a sighted one, and all students learned sign language, thus embracing the pain of separation for the deaf while having pyramids of fun.

By the end of the first year, classes had grown from twenty to two hundred, about one-third of whom were disabled and underprivileged students. In six years two thousand youngsters were enrolled.

Some people asked, "Why a not-for-profit organization?"

"Because you can't put a dollar sign on a little person looking up at you saying, 'I did it,'" replied Deby, a spunky forty-year-old who dances as she talks.

Soon the backyard operation moved to an old grocery store in North Fresno. Students and parents pitched in, tossing out shelving and tearing down walls.

In 1987 the first Barrier Breakers team was formed. The sixty-member team performs to music with a message. It's the only group of its kind in the nation.

The enthusiastic, noncompetitive team tumbles, flips, vaults, trampolines, and rolls its way right into the hearts of the audience, earning a standing ovation, tears, and awe.

Since its first performance for a local Rotary Club conference, the team has entertained at sports halftimes and at state, national, and international events.

"We show them how it can be—able ones lifting others out of wheelchairs. It's a dance," said the leading lady, dressed in a bright blue jogging suit.

Able-bodied students learn to believe in the unbelievable and to follow their hearts. "Many become teachers and counselors," said Deby, introducing Jennifer Bass, a sixteen-year old who has been taking classes for six years.

"I like to perform, not compete," Jennifer said, still out of breath from a balance beam workout.

When the Barrier Breakers demonstrate at events where able-bodied teams are also performing, both teams win praise.

But when the team with wheelchairs and crutches takes its bow, the audience says more than "Good job." People say, "Amazing!" "Inspirational." "I will never forget you!" "You gave me a lot to think about."

"The teenagers who come here say they would rather be a part of this because it is life-changing," said Deby, director and one of thirty-three trainers who staff the gym.

Her dream is still evolving. "Now that we are accepted in our community, the next step is to move into the world with the message," said Deby.

In every performance the message is pure and simple: Able-bodied and disabled belong together. Deby makes it even more clear.

"The Bible says to go out and bring in the blind, the lame, and the crippled. I think that passage should finish with . . . so they can teach us about life,'" she said.

Kids: The Heart of Community

In May 1995 we were on hand for Awards Day at Brownlow Elementary School, an urban, multicultural neighborhood school in Knoxville, Tennessee. This year's awards theme was "Only in America."

Excitement was in the air. A father scooped his young son from the car and skipped with him into the old gym where 120 parents, friends, and Brownlow students awaited the entrance of the Brownlow Cowgirls Line Dance Team.

In the schoolyard a beehive of whispering third-grade girls buzzed around their teacher for last-minute instructions.

"Pull your hat strings tight, tuck in your blouses, straighten your scarves, and you kids look great," she said with a half-smile.

Then Ray Charles' version of "The Star-Spangled Banner" began. All eyes turned to watch the Brownlow Cowgirls march in from the back of the gym, their wide-brimmed hats and red bandanas all in a line. Holding flags, they marched down the center aisle, halting in the front of the gym where the awards were about to begin.

But first, the dance. As the music shifted to a country beat, the cowgirls swung onto the old wooden floor. One step up, two steps back, clap. Heads to the left, moving in the line, kick and stomp. Some looked serious. Others beamed, trying not to laugh. Stomp, stomp, all bow.

On this special day, students were permitted to wear their shirts inside out. Priceless was a first-grade girl, white shoulder pads flapping like wings from her purple T-shirt as she walked up proudly to receive the Most Improved Student Award.

All summer long, we have gathered heartfelt stories about the joy and positive impact of children. Near Glacier National Park, in Polson, Montana, we were hooked by the work of first graders at Cherry Valley School. Colorful fish mobiles dangling above the desk at the post office lured us to meet with JeNeil Devlin, the first grade teacher.

Several years ago JeNeil asked the postmaster if her class might decorate the post office for National Education Week. The community, delighted, asked the pupils to decorate it permanently.

"Seeing this is good for those who don't get into the schools. The Senior Citizens especially like the project," said the postal clerk.

"The town's favorite display is How to Cook a Turkey," said JeNeil. In November, students give a variety of cooking instructions complete with illustrations—guaranteed to tantalize your appetite and tickle your spirit. No matter where we go across this great nation, we keep learning the same lesson: Teachers plus students equal community. And that's something to cheer about.

13

Go the Distance

My mother once told me that as a child I was afraid of everything, even flies. It's true! I began this journey with a low tolerance for annoying things—the sound of eighteen-wheelers barreling down interstate highways when I'm trying to use a pay phone, the curse of dive-bombing mosquitoes in campground showers, and warning signs such as WATCH FOR RATTLESNAKES, Welcome to Texas.

However, the goodness of people whose lives touched ours daily and the beauty of bountiful America offer a mighty strong counterbalance, even for this Campfire Girl who never lit a fire. I've changed.

A true dream, that is to say, one that lands on earth because it is fished out of the sky, has a life and purpose of its own. It was easy to see, after only a few interviews, that the real journey—the journey into the hearts and souls of fellow Americans—would never be over. So, too, is this true for those who "go the distance."

Destination: Jobs

Wow, do we have stuff—two boxes of books we thought we couldn't live without, two fishing poles never cast, two sleeping bags used once, and a Coleman camping stove that hasn't been lit.

Though we pared down to a very slim twenty-six-foot household, we still have more than we need. This reminds us of our interview with Jeff Hardin, a Minneapolis businessman and volunteer for a project called Destination: Jobs. The people of Minneapolis discovered they, too, had what they needed, right in their own backyard.

In the last decade ninety-eight percent of all job growth in the Minneapolis metropolitan area was in the suburbs, with seventy-five percent of that in the outer-ring suburbs.

Meanwhile, the unemployment rate for people living in the central city exceeded fifteen percent compared with the overall rate of about four percent.

"Something had to be done to get the people who needed jobs out to where the employers needed them," said Hardin, a tall, lanky man with a background in human resources.

In 1990 the city of Minneapolis provided funds for a social service agency to run a van out to the suburbs where there was no other reliable transportation. The plan was called Reverse Commute. For a while it worked, but the problem was far more complex than mere transportation.

The problem would require a collaborative effort to co-ordinate social, economic, and personal factors to confront bigger issues: poverty, urban blight, increased unemployment, and the consequences—crime and drugs. Government was not able to manage this.

"The key to unlocking this door of despair is meaningful work," said Hardin, pounding a gentle fist on the table. "Work that provides adequate income, health benefits, dignity, and self-respect."

In 1992 five Minneapolis metropolitan groups met to take a deeper look. They included suburban employers, government agencies, Chambers of Commerce, training and employment agencies, and the transit authorities. Together they spearheaded a massive plan to educate themselves and to boost job training programs.

Thus Reverse Commute became Destination: Jobs, a much larger project aimed at changing attitudes, erasing prejudices, and allowing vulnerability on all sides.

The urban poor faced differences in culture, language, and workstyles. The suburban elite faced doubt, uncertainty, and rigid thinking. And volunteers had to accept that this would be another job they wouldn't be paid for and for which someone else would take the credit.

"You can't just agree with the logic. 'It's a good idea,' won't go far. You have to fight for the success of the program. And business has a show-me attitude. It's their resistance to change," said Hardin.

The program kicked off in 1993 with a Job Fair. It was a central event, a place for implementation to begin and a forum for business and prospective employees to meet after months of preparation. But two weeks before the big event, only twenty businesses were signed up.

"I had to twist arms and beg," Hardin said. "Finally, forty-four did come."

It was a moving experience. Although the Job Fair was held in a suburban shopping mall, the suburbanites—with less than one percent minority population—were anxious. When the first busload of diverse people showed up, the county commissioner and the mayor were there to greet them.

"Then a black counselor started to cry, and we all realized how much it took for these people to get on that bus," said Hardin. "Some put their arms around each other, and we all knew this program was more than just jobs."

The second annual Job Fair was held in 1994. Hardin still had to twist arms. But the third year was a charm. Radisson Hotel sent a bus to help with the crowd.

Though Destination: Jobs has become a model for other cities to learn from, indeed it is much more. Hardin says, "The real success is that it changed us."

Serious Fun Runs Her Life

Imagine angel wings lifting you and carrying you up. That's the feeling Christine Lindblad of Boca Raton, Florida, remembers at the victory dinner in Washington D.C., after running the twenty-first annual Marine Corps Marathon in October 1996.

Dressed in a Leukemia Society T-shirt, running shorts, and spit-clean sneakers, Chris jogged us through what it took to become a serious runner. But more serious are the facts about leukemia, she says.

More than 48,000 Americans will die from leukemia or a related cancer this year. It is the leading disease killer of children, and it strikes ten times more adults than children. "The good news is that three-fourths of the money raised by the Leukemia Society goes directly to research," she said.

Chris ran the marathon to encourage Leena, a seven-year old with Hodgkins disease, and to bolster her own ailing self-image after her divorce.

"I read an ad in the local newspapers and went to an informational meeting," she said.

That's how the thirty-two-year old took the leap, joining the Leukemia Society of America's Team in Training program.

"When I saw what these people were doing for others, I decided to go for it," she said, referring to the camaraderie,

218

rigorous fitness and training schedules, and a partner to pace through wind and stormy weather.

"The hardest were three twenty-mile practice runs," she said. But the process is well worth the outcome.

Christine Lindblad of Boca Raton is proud to have run the Marine Corps Marathon in 1996 to raise money for the Leukemia Society.

"I never thought anything could compare to having my kids," Chris said. "Running a marathon comes close. It's a kind of birthing process."

Organizing her active six- and eight-year-old children was another challenge. "At first they complained, but when I showed them Leena's picture, they jumped on their bikes and pedaled along," she said.

At the pasta dinner held the evening before the marathon, Chris met Leena. She paused to show us the wristband she wore during the marathon with Leena's name, age, and diagnosis on it.

"I made a commitment to raise $2,800 dollars. It was easier for me to run the twenty-six miles than to ask people for donations."

But she did it. She pressed through her shyness and learned to believe in herself and the power to get things to happen. More than a hundred people made donations.

"I even got my ex-husband to sponsor me," she said, smiling.

As we spoke, Chris flipped through her photo album. "The starting line was two miles long. We began at Arlington, ran around the Pentagon, through Georgetown and looped back again," she said, her finger tracing a map. "We had to cross the 14th Street Bridge by a certain time or ride the stragglers' bus."

Some sixteen thousand runners circled the nation's monuments that day. The only crisis came toward the end. At Mile 20, the Marines ran out of Gatorade. At Mile 22, one of Chris's legs started cramping. She was dehydrating. Fueled by pure determination, she limped through Arlington Cemetery and up the last hill toward the finish line, pale-faced and puffing.

"I thought the last part, where the crowd is cheering us on, would be the easiest," she said. "It was the hardest."

Then her partner Stephanie Ball from Palm Beach Shores reached out a hand, and they flew past the finish line together. Five hours and thirty-nine minutes of hitting the pavement was over.

"I was in tears. I kept saying, 'I did it. I did it.' I felt so good about myself. I made a commitment and stuck with it."

For the next week, Chris wore the plastic bracelet with Leena's name on it. "My race was over, but Leena was still running," she said.

On Call for Twenty Years

A career choice should be a healthy expression of one's skills, abilities, and God-given talents. Otherwise, one's life purpose can be frustrated, even lost.

We sat in the Downieville Diner, munching on English muffins and conducting a one-question survey: What's special about Frank Lang, the nurse practitioner who has been the only medical provider in western Sierra County, California, for twenty-some years?

A retired veterinarian said, "Frank has so much experience. He doesn't put up a front, and he's clear about who he is and what he can do. He's also a good banjo picker."

Linc, a retired mortician, continued, "On a routine twenty-dollar visit, Frank found that I needed a new heart valve. He sent me to Reno to have it checked out, and for $2,000 they told me that Frank was right. Another time, Frank told me he thought he could help me if I stopped smoking. Otherwise, we were wasting our time."

Trusting in Frank's wisdom, Linc stopped smoking.

Carlo, owner of the local pizzeria, said, "The average urban physician has only seven minutes to spend with each patient. You might as well call a priest! We are so lucky to have Frank."

How did Frank choose nursing, and how did he come to practice in a tiny mountain town?

In high school his ACT scores showed a strong aptitude for science. Not sure about that, he decided to study accounting, but he soon discovered how disinterested he was "in finding those missing two cents."

Things began adding up in 1962 when Frank joined the U.S. Air Force, took another battery of career tests, and scored high in the medical sciences. Frank became a corpsman in a field hospital. It was challenging work, and he learned about emergency care, but he wasn't yet satisfied.

"I could see a disparity between the function of a corpsman, which is similar to today's paramedic, and the role of the nurse, who was mostly doing administration and paperwork," he said. "Why wasn't the nurse trained to do the more skilled work?"

In 1966 when his active duty ended, Frank began dreaming up the role of the highly trained R.N. who could work independently in remote settings: the nurse practitioner. He stayed on track, married Bette Jo, an R.N., and entered the nursing program at the University of Northern Colorado.

After graduation he worked in the Army Nurse Corps at Walter Reed Army Hospital for a year, then transferred back to Denver. There, he finished his master's degree at the University of Colorado in 1973 and went to work for the University, helping to develop the role of the N.P.

His dream came true. In 1976 the couple and their three sons flew to Downieville, population 325, to see about a position with the U.S. Public Health Service.

"The board hired me, although we took a cut in pay," Frank told us. "We said we'd be here for two years. But at the end of two years there was nobody else to take the job, so we stayed—for twenty more years."

Frank's career choice has influenced thousands of people, including one very dear to his heart—his son, J. R., who has become a family practitioner. In the summer, when the tourist population of Downieville and the surrounding rural areas swells from 1,500 to several thousand, Frank gets some relief. J. R. comes home to spell his dad for a month.

Did Frank ever wish he had become a physician?

"No, It's like the Robert Frost poem," he said. "I chose this road, and my life is better for having done it."

Though Frank loves working with the high-tech medical database that links the clinic to resources in Sacramento and Reno, he says, "I also love the ordinary time, the opportunity to develop the nurse-patient relationship."

Recently, something extraordinary happened that took the calm man by surprise. He was chosen to receive the Nurse Practitioner of the Year Award given by the National Health Service Corps "for dedication to the improvement of the health of the nation's underserved populations." The award was presented in April 1998, at the NHSC twenty-fifth anniversary celebration in Washington, D.C.

This is a happy story, but it might not have been this way. In 1947, when Frank was five, his family emigrated from Holland to the U.S. Had they stayed in Europe, Frank says he probably would have had no choice regarding a career. He would have been a coal miner.

The people of Sierra County are convinced that this would have been a terrible loss.

Someone to Watch Over Me

Ruth Neubert of Sierra City, California, always knew about the Big Sister organization, but she never thought about joining. Then she heard an advertisement on television about how the organization desperately needed volunteers. So at sixty, Ruth became a Big Sister.

"I didn't discuss it with any of my friends," Ruth said, rolling her gray-blue eyes. "I didn't want anyone to talk me out of it or say I was too old or try to warn me that I could get a terrible kid."

Then her own mind began pelting her with negatives. Surely, she hadn't been the perfect parent. Did she have the time to volunteer?

"I didn't let that stop me either," she said.

At an informal meeting, Ruth learned that being a Big Sister meant making a one-year commitment to spend four hours a week with a Little Sister. She would also have to pass a psychological test.

When someone from Big Sisters called to schedule an appointment for an interview and a psychological exam, she had second thoughts. "Am I too old for this?" But she still went to the interview.

Periodically, someone called to say the Big Sisters were trying to match Ruth with a child. Finally, five months later, she got the clinching call.

"An eleven-year-old girl from a disadvantaged home said that age didn't matter to her," Ruth said. "All she wanted was a friend."

Ruth met Trina, her Little Sister, at the McDonald's close to where Trina lived.

"I still have a picture of this beautiful child with reddish-blonde hair and blue eyes sitting across from me," Ruth said. "The first thing she asked me was, did I notice a problem with her one eye? I hadn't."

"This one shoots off into left field," Trina said. "We are on welfare, and the doctor said we aren't covered, and he can't do anything for me."

After Trina shared her concern, she said no more about it. She listened as Ruth rattled off a litany of possible places where she thought Trina might like to go. Trina seemed like a happy child. She was easy to talk to.

When Ruth finished, Trina said, "One of the first things I'd like to do is make chocolate chip cookies. I've never done that."

Soon Ruth discovered that Trina's eye problem was more than cosmetic. Due to her injured eye muscle, she was behind in school. Ruth started to tutor Trina in her schoolwork.

One day while Ruth was visiting with a friend, she casually mentioned that she had become a Big Sister and that her Little Sister had a medical problem that should be corrected. Her friend happened to be the president of the Sweet Water Women's Club in Bonita, California.

A few weeks later, Ruth's friend called. The service club wanted to help Trina. Could Ruth investigate the exact cost of the operation and make the arrangements?

"I called the doctor and negotiated a price," Ruth said, with a smile that reflected that victorious day. "And when the surgery was done, Trina delivered a magnificent thank-you speech to all the ladies at a luncheon."

During the four years that Trina and Ruth met as Big and Little Sisters, they went to lots of plays and Ruth discovered that Trina had acting talent. So Ruth enrolled Trina in a summer acting/theater class. Trina also became an agile ice skater during those years they shared together. But there were also tough times.

Early one cold, rainy Saturday, Trina called Ruth. "We're out in the mud. We've been evicted again," she said. Ruth told Trina that she would be right there. Then she called a friend to help out with the unfortunate family.

"I brought Trina to my house, made her a warm breakfast, and got her into dry clothes. Then we called her grandmother and arranged for Trina and her brother to stay with their grandparents until their mother found a new home." Over the years, Trina and Ruth have stayed in touch. Trina is married now. She has a little girl of her own and lives in Idaho.

Does volunteering make a difference? "I noticed the last time Trina brought her daughter to visit, that she is a wonderful mother," Ruth said.

The Children's Defense Fund

"When it looked like the sun wasn't gonna shine anymore, God put a rainbow in the clouds," sang Maya Angelou, mistress of ceremonies for the Beat the Odds, 1998 Awards Program and Dinner held in March at the Los Angeles Convention Center.

The Children's Defense Fund is celebrating its twenty-fifth year of standing for children. It began the summer of 1973, when Marian Wright Edelman launched a children's movement to give voice to those who cannot vote—America's poor, minority, and disabled children.

The private, nonprofit organization—one that doesn't accept government funds—builds healthy communities, boosts families through educational programs, and lobbies for equal opportunity and social justice.

"If you hadn't asked me to be here tonight, I'd be picketing out there," said Angelou, the poet laureate, who read one of her poems at President Clinton's inauguration in 1993. Today, Angelou, dressed in a red linen suit and wearing pearl earrings and a matching necklace, hugged Edelman, a shorter woman with similar stature. Then she opened her arms to the crowd.

"We are honored to have a distinguished guest with us tonight," she said in her melodious baritone voice. "Rosa Parks, the woman whose shoulders we all stand on."

We jumped to our feet, clapping for the tiny African-American woman who, in December of 1955 refused to give up her seat to a white man, sparking the Montgomery [Alabama] bus boycott. Now hunched over in a wheelchair, she raised her head, and with gleaming eyes, waved, and smiled at the thousand-plus crowd.

"Strength of character is what makes the difference in facing adversity," Angelou said, introducing the first of five high school students in the Los Angeles area to be honored at the national convention's kick-off dinner. "Let's see how Erin Tucker beat the odds."

The lights dimmed, and the banquet hall hushed. In awe, we watched five short video stories depicting a day in the life of each teen and how he or she overcame misfortune with the help of a mentor—a caring sister, a guidance counselor, the director of an after-school program.

It was like the TV show *Queen for a Day* but better. These youths weren't getting new refrigerators and fancy trips. They were getting computers and a college education —a future, thanks to big-time contributors like Sony Pictures Entertainment and Universal Studios, Inc.

While presenting the awards, TV actress, Victoria Rowell, who plays on *Diagnosis Murder*, told how she grew up as a ward of the state.

"I learned I could be strong and beat the odds with intelligence and dignity," she told us. "I did this because someone stood up for me."

Edelman summarized this portion of the evening with her favorite line: "Nobody has the right to give up on any child." We were all wiping our eyes with the table napkins.

Then Edelman, the woman nobody can say no to, the trailblazer who back in the 1960s got U.S. Senator Bobby Kennedy to visit the poorest ghettos of the Deep South, presented the final award.

"This year's Leadership Award goes to the hippest man—most generous friend, proud father, producer, composer, multimedia entrepreneur, and long-distance runner who stays on the leading edge—Quincy Jones."

Jones, winner of twenty-six Grammy Awards and an Emmy Award for his score of the opening episode of the landmark TV miniseries, *Roots*, was given a wooden plaque engraved with a children's prayer: *Dear Lord, be good to me. The sea is so wide and my boat is so small.*

"This is one of the most meaningful awards I have ever received," he said. "My family moved to the south side of Chicago in 1943. It was the largest ghetto in America during the eye of the depression. The odds were stacked against me. Luckily, I found someone who taught me what music is about. I was fortunate. Lionel Hampton, Ray Charles, and others took me under their wings."

Angelou, a true "rainbow in the clouds," who has mentored multitudes, whispered into the microphone these final words of wisdom:

"Learn to be quiet enough to hear the tenacity and drive in others so you can hear it in yourself."

Rearview Miracles

S tories that heal and guide our lives must include
life's adversities. For it is not what happens in life,
but how we respond to what happens that renders
our personal story soulful. And letting go of the fear that
surrounds adversity is easier if we believe ourselves to be a
part of a larger, cosmic story. Thus, despair transforms to
hope and doubt to faith. Then by faith, our cry in the
darkness is heard, a new story takes form, and life spirals on.

In retrospect, one would think that life is simply meant
to be this way.

Mickey's Story

When her husband left her stranded in Mesa, Arizona, and headed for California and a new life with another woman, Mickey Lemaster felt totally lost. On the surface her life looked grim, but beneath the pain, something wonderful was stirring.

"I kept saying, 'God has things happen for a reason.' I just couldn't find the reason," said Mickey. "All I knew was that I had to do something, but I didn't know what."

Though Mickey was staying with her girlfriend, she felt homeless—a feeling strikingly similar to how she felt years ago when her first husband was killed by a drunk driver, and she was left alone to raise two young children.

"Then I realized Mesa has a lot of homeless people. So I went down to the shelter and asked what I could do," she said.

Her assignment was distributing clothes, but more importantly, it was her introduction to working with the poor.

"I was so fulfilled there," she said.

Two months later, an apologetic John returned, asking Mickey to take him back. She decided it was worth a try. They would begin with a camping trip into Mexico.

Mickey had mixed feelings about leaving her job, but she found an answer. Because the homeless center had a surplus of used clothing, Mickey offered to take a truckload to the poor in Mexico. John and Mickey left Mesa with a pickup full of hand-me-downs and hopeful hearts.

In Mexico they met a man selling ironwood carvings. He had five daughters and a son. The youngest child, the son, had a heart condition and was about to have major surgery. Mickey and John went to their home to meet the family and deliver clothing.

The family lived in a humble dwelling with a dirt floor. The walls were made of tall, straight cactus. Three of the walls were shared with other families. In the center of the one-room home was a truck wheel that served as their stove.

After Mickey and John emptied much of the clothing, Mickey went into their camper for other items she knew the family needed: a set of dishes, cooking pots, and a frying pan. Then she reached deeper, giving each girl a baby doll from her treasured collection.

"When John saw me give away my best Cabbage Patch Kid, he became a believer," Mickey said. "I don't know who was touched more—me, the children, or John."

Mickey's work with the poor continued.

The following year, she went on an eight-day mission to Jamaica with a South Dakota medical team. Her church sponsored the trip. Since Mickey had no medical training, she joined the team as a "hugger and rocker" and was assigned to the pediatric clinic.

The first day, Mickey noticed a three-pound premature infant with severe diaper rash. Everyone, including the child's mother, had given up on her, but not Mickey. She asked to be assigned to her.

Mickey rocked and hugged and fed and loved the baby.

"She was on a four-hour feeding schedule, regurgitating the food, not gaining weight and bound to die. I floated the child in water, simulating the feeling of being in the womb, and placed her on frequent small feedings," she said.

Within twenty-four hours, the child was responding. Mickey also taught the baby's mother how to care for her child, reassuring her it would work. For Mickey, too, had been the mother of a three-pound infant thirty years ago, her daughter Kim.

While Mickey rocked "Baby Jamaica," she began to reminisce.

"Kim was born one year after her brother. I wasn't ready for another child, certainly not a preemie," she said. "I was overwhelmed and frightened."

Eleven months later, when Mickey's first husband died in an auto accident, all-consuming fear plummeted to deep sorrow.

"As I look back, I think I never fully welcomed my own child," Mickey said.

After the medical mission to Jamaica, Mickey flew back to Oklahoma where she and her husband now lived and met an unexpected gift. When she got off the plane, Kim was there to greet her, not Mickey's husband as she had expected.

"How perfect that was! I embraced her and couldn't stop crying," Mickey said with joyful tears. "Something inside me was healed."

Missouri Duo's Mission: Old Churches

In Texas the wide-open spaces are runways for jetting winds that whip across vast fields where cattle graze. With my head bowed, I carry a basket of dirty clothes, a box of Ultra Fab, and a jug of Clorox, aiming toward the warm sanctuary of the laundry room at the KOA campground in Amarillo. That's where I met Norman and Arlene Price, who were folding a mountain of worn-out towels and several hills of faded work clothes.

Eight years ago, Norman and Arlene began volunteering part time with a group called Campers on Mission, restoring new life to old churches.

"It was so spiritually rewarding that we decided we wanted to do this kind of work full time," Arlene said.

Then, as if Arlene handed him the baton, Norman began to speak. "So we started buying tools, such as a power nailer, a saw, and a hammer, as if that's what was going to happen," he said.

And it did.

In October 1994 Norman was laid off from his job. Although he had other offers because he was known as a hard worker, Arlene urged him not to accept them.

Soon the Prices received a phone call from the Missouri Baptist Builders, asking them to put a roof on a children's home in East Prairie, Missouri. Their new life had begun.

"It's all free labor. I place the shingles, and Norman pounds the nails," said Arlene.

"We don't accept any money for the work, just a meal here and there and sometimes a little help with our truck," Norman added.

"When we left Missouri, we had $200, a 1981 Ford pickup, a 1977 fifth-wheel camper, and a 1986 Sprint that we pulled behind the rig," Arlene said.

"All of them wore out," Norman laughed, ending that round.

Somehow, things would just even out for the busy full-timers. One time the happy carpenters installed a new roof on an old church near Phoenix, Arizona. Just as they were finishing the job, a man in the congregation noticed the couple's rattletrap truck and offered his mechanical help.

"The truck came back all repaired, and the congregation took up a collection for us—exactly $200," Arlene said, smiling at her partner.

Beneath their faith stands a heartwarming foundation of abiding love. Norman met Arlene when he was a teenager. He was her student. Arlene was the country schoolmarm who taught grades one through eight in Prairie Point, Missouri. She was nineteen and married at that time.

Eight years later, Norman showed up at Arlene's doorstep to show off his shiny new car. "My family was poor, and we never had a new car. Now that I was working, I had something to be proud of," Norman said.

Arlene, now twenty-six and the mother of three children, was happy for Norman's success, though she herself was in a failing situation.

"My husband was an alcoholic, and that was the year he drank himself to death," she said.

When Norman stepped into her life to help out, what was once a student-teacher relationship blossomed into a lasting marriage. He adopted Arlene's children as his own and sold his new car to make a down payment on a better home for his family.

"Everybody said it wouldn't last because of the seven-year age difference," said Arlene, smiling. That was thirty-six years ago.

"There is one thing you really have to give up when you give your life to the Lord," Norman said, switching back to today's volunteer project. "It's pride," he said, shaking his head.

When Norman sacrificed his new car to help his new bride and her family, he demonstrated that lesson, or so I thought. But that's not what he was talking about.

"You have to let others give to you," he said. "Because my family had very little money, that was a sore spot for me. I am able to make money, but I would rather work for God," Norman explained.

Arlene is simply a woman of faith. God sent her just the right help thirty-six years ago, so why wouldn't He keep providing? "God takes care of the birds. Why not us?" she said.

Are You Happy?

Over and over we are asked: Are you happy?

After nine months of living and working on the road, we had learned some things about happiness. It's more about *being* than about *having*, and it's always connected to the resiliency of the human heart.

In mid-December we were camped in New Port Beach, California, south of Los Angeles. Late one afternoon we were walking on Crystal Cove Beach. Bruce was snapping shots of running sandpipers, gliding sea gulls, and swooping pelicans. I noticed there were no shells on the beach as there had been on northern California's rugged coast where we had filled our pockets with treasures—round, smooth stones, bits of driftwood, and tiny shells.

What was present on this warmer shore were colors and sounds: the emerald, tough-skinned prickly pear cactus, the iridescent green watercolors that swish across the sand while waves of blue wash to shore, and the awesome sound of dashing walls of water where only surfers dare to go. Things that could not be collected, only savored.

That evening we drove to Laguna Beach for dinner, but we decided it was too pricey. We stopped at Albertson's grocery store and secured a small feast for half the price. I tossed spaghetti in extra garlic while Bruce listened to the news and the hum of the stove fan.

It was an uneventful night until 1:30 A.M. when an unexpected wind whipped off the ocean, flapping our awning and delivering torrents of rain. Within minutes, the awning buckled under the weight of the water, shaking our home-on-wheels and waking us.

Together we struggled to open the door, tearing the canvas awning. Barefooted and dancing in the rain, we laughed. We had not lost our happiness.

The next day we drove to Santa Monica to visit one of my high school friends who was visiting her Uncle Frank and Aunt Mary. They had a story to tell.

In March 1995, Frank had his second open heart surgery. This time it was to replace an artery. "Right in here," he said, pointing to his abdomen. The blood was not circulating to Frank's legs. "That's why Dr. McCarthy opened me up," he said.

It was then that McCarthy discovered how occluded the eighty-year-old Italian man's artery had become. While rerouting the vessel, Frank's heart stopped.

"My husband's heart was literally in the doctor's hand when it stopped beating," Mary said. The determined physician massaged Frank's heart, keeping the patient alive for nearly twenty-five minutes. Then, thinking it was futile, McCarthy finally gave up.

"The doctor was closing me up when my heart started beating again," Frank said with a grin.

McCarthy was not sure Frank would be all right. He took Mary into a private room and closed the door. "'You'd better sit down,' he began. He told me all that happened, and it took him fifteen minutes to tell me what I wanted to know—that he thought Frank would be all right," said Frank's tearful wife. "It's the best thing I ever heard."

But Frank did not awaken right away. His family was encouraged to talk to him. His daughter, Shirley, was the one who said, "If you can hear us, Dad, wiggle your toes."

"Up went his toes," Mary said. "The kids were screaming, and I was crying."

The doctor came in and asked Frank orientation questions—his name and birthday. There was no response. Finally, the parish priest came in to give him the last rites—just in case Frank wasn't coming back.

"I couldn't talk yet, but I kept thinking, 'They got the wrong guy,'" Frank said.

Hours later, when he was fully awake and able to talk, Frank asked his priest why he had lived. His reply was simple. "He thinks I have a lot of work to do yet—like helping with the kids."

As Frank spoke to us, his nine-month-old great-granddaughter Angelina slept on his chest, perfectly content to be with her grandpa. Isn't it interesting that this child called Angel arrived just as Frank was released from the hospital? We guess Great-grandpa just has to stick around.

Stories like these answer the question, "Are you happy?" The answer is yes—both on the inside where happiness cannot be rattled and on the outside where we can see the joyful workings of the human heart.

Becky McKee's Opus

Becky McKee of University Heights, Ohio, had taught physical education to elementary, junior high, and college students for twenty-two years. She loved being a teacher—until 1992 when she was assaulted twice in one year by inner city girls. Not waiting for three strikes, she declared herself out.

"I had to ask myself, did I really want to keep putting myself in this situation?" she said. "Worst of all, I thought I was getting someplace with the kids."

Becky left teaching kids and became a personal trainer for adults for three years. But something was missing in her life. Then she saw *Mr. Holland's Opus*, a movie about a music teacher who thinks teaching is going to be easy. After becoming disillusioned, Holland falls in love with the students and the magic of the educational process.

"It hit me really hard," she said recalling her tears. "As I left the theater, all I could think was, 'I'm a teacher. I want to teach kids.'"

The next day, while walking in the woods, Becky said aloud, "Okay, God, I really love hiking and working with kids." Then she threw up her hands and asked, "How is this going to happen?"

A few days later she got the answer. While browsing through the classified ads in an outdoor education magazine, she spied an ad for the Catherine B. Freer Wilderness

Therapy Group in Oregon. Altogether there were thirteen qualifications. "I wadded it up and threw it in the corner of the room," she said. "I had twelve qualifications. I thought I needed all of them."

But when a friend suggested that Becky call and just ask a few questions, the eager teacher grabbed the phone and called the program director. The teaching position was in a drug and alcohol treatment program for recovering adolescents. She sent her resume.

"That was exactly thirteen days from the time I saw *Mr. Holland's Opus*," Becky said, still amazed how fast things happened.

Soon she received an offer to do an internship, which she accepted with one stipulation—that she could bring Perry, her half border collie, half German shepherd puppy along.

That's how Becky, her puppy, and two other staff members led seven troubled adolescents into the wilderness for three weeks in the summer of 1996.

Four of the seven youths came straight from juvenile detention. They didn't choose to be there, and in the beginning none of them were really present.

"When you see these kids—look into their eyes. There's nobody home," the teacher told us.

The program is designed to push participants to their physical and emotional limits. They hike six to eight hours a day carrying forty-pound packs and work on issues that all adolescents have to deal with—anger, sexuality, self-esteem, authority. In the evening, they sit around the campfire in two hours of group therapy.

University Heights, Ohio, teacher Becky McKee and her dog Perry work together to help teens change the direction of their lives.

"It presses them to explore why they are doing drugs," Becky said. "By the end of the second week, they were able to absorb what we were working on."

Part of the outdoor experience was the three-day solo. Each adolescent was sent into the wilderness to face his or her fears, armed only with art supplies and a journal.

One student who rekindled Becky's fear of being assaulted again was a young man with a violent temper. "My instinct was to stay away from him, but Perry's instinct was to get closer," she said. Her dog would lay his head on the camper having the most difficult time.

This particular teen did the most work, changed the most, and was able to articulate what he learned, restoring Becky's faith in kids to see both sides—the angry adolescent who can be violent and the scared teenager wanting guidance.

In twenty-one days, the spirit of teaching returned to the teacher, and clarity of mind returned to the students' eyes. Face to face with troubled teens, Becky discovered how much she missed teaching. So when she was offered a contract to teach in the wilderness program, she said, "Great!"

Lifesaving Disappointment

Often stories of faith and hope come wrapped in strange packages, later identified as gifts from above. Sometimes a rumpled corner, like a glitch in the plan, is a subtle clue that tells us there's something special inside.

Christina Faulkner and her husband Andy were planning to meet some college friends for a long weekend of camping. The couples hadn't seen each other in three years. The Faulkners live in Noblesville, Indiana, and their friends live in Virginia. They would meet halfway.

"But our friends called the night before and said not to come," Christina said. "The campground was flooded."

Christina, her husband, and their two kids were terribly disappointed.

"We were all packed and ready to go. Andy even took extra time off work," she said.

The next day, since they were not camping, Christina and her spouse went to their four-year-old son's swimming lesson. While sitting by the pool watching little ones dog-paddle and pass pollywog tests, Christina's eyes were drawn to a child's head bobbing up and down in the water. With each bob, Christina was more anxious.

"His eyes came out of the water, but not his mouth," she said.

When Christina asked Andy if he thought the child was in trouble, he said, "He looks fine to me."

Andy thought she was referring to their son Alex.

Then Christina said with alarm, "He's not okay!"

Fully clothed, she jumped into the pool and fished out the gasping child.

"It happened so fast," she said. "Nobody was watching."

While washing the dishes after lunch, Christina became tearful.

"We weren't supposed to be camping three hundred miles away. We were meant to be at that swimming lesson," she said. "I'm so glad that's where we were."

15

Mixed Blessings

A ccepting life's bittersweet realities is more than tough. It's the challenge of unconditional love. Like heartburn, emotional pain sits like a lump of uncertainty until compassion, the deepest feeling of all, washes away the anger, dissolves the fear, and softens the hardened heart.

Most uncanny is to discover, after the fact, that perhaps you were guided right into the storm, equipped with precisely what was needed all along.

Life Is Like a Box of Chocolates

"When people with schizophrenia get off track, they live in a world where they think everyone else is crazy, leaving them with a sense of total isolation," Terry Polnasek said.

She was speaking about her brother. "When Jeff is on medication, he does pretty well, but he always needs our love," she said.

Terry is the youngest of seven children. As a child, she looked up to her brothers Steve and Jeff, who called her "Nertz." When Terry was in junior high school, Jeff was a senior at the University of Wisconsin in Madison. He was an honor student until tragedy struck. Steve, the older brother, died in a car accident.

"Jeff's grades dropped, he stopped bathing, and started saying crazy things," Terry recalls. She was confused about Jeff's strange behavior and angry that he was getting all the attention when the whole family was grieving over Steve.

Jeff was soon hospitalized for psychiatric evaluation and placed on medication. It helped, but when their father died, Jeff relapsed, and Terry's life turned upside down. Since all four of her sisters were grown, that left just Jeff, Terry, and her mother living at home.

"Jeff and I fought furiously," Terry said. "I had no compassion for his illness. One day when I was sitting on the floor playing with my little nephew, my mother noticed how happy I was and whispered in my ear, 'That's how I feel about Jeff.'"

But that kind of love didn't sink in until her mother died.

"I think I finally embraced Jeff as my brother because my mother never told us that it was our responsibility to care for him after she died," Terry said.

"But I still worried that nobody would help and that I would be overwhelmed by his illness."

After college Terry worked for a while in Wisconsin, then moved to Cleveland, Ohio, because of her job.

"That's when I felt a shift in my anger," she said. "I started blaming my sisters for my upset, which gave me space to get to know Jeff."

Terry began writing letters and making long distance phone calls to her brother—creating a relationship she once thought was impossible. She even invited Jeff to Cleveland for a visit and helped him arrange to get there. "I enjoyed taking him around to visit my friends," Terry said. "I began to admire him for all he had been through."

Then something magical happened. After seeing the movie *Forrest Gump*, one sister called to say that she too could see the simplistic beauty in their brother. It was a beginning.

But not until something terrible happened did the sisters bond closer together. While attending a friend's wedding in Wisconsin, Terry received a phone call: Jeff was missing.

"He had stopped taking his medication because it didn't come in the mail," said Terry. "He was talking crazy, threw everything out of his apartment, and just started walking."

When the police found Jeff at a discount store, he had a jar of peanut butter in his pocket, some McDonald's wrappers, and a razor for shaving.

"He was lost and trying to find a job," Terry said. "At least he was able to ask the police to please call his sisters."

When his sisters came to get him, Jeff was at his worst. He was unkempt, underweight, and talking to mirrors. They took him to one of the sisters' homes to try doing a family intervention.

"My nieces and nephews had never seen Jeff in this condition. They got a glimpse of what Jeff has to deal with," Terry said.

Jeff, who was "naturally polite and would never harm anyone," was paranoid and confused. "Why have you called the cops on me?" he kept asking.

Terry wept as she looked into her brother's eyes.

"Jeff, there is a space between you and me. I can't get in that space, and you can't either. This is the best we can do, and we do love you," she said.

Jeff spent the next six months in a psychiatric hospital adjusting to his medication and regaining his confidence. Today he lives in a halfway house in Wisconsin. Recently, he flew to Laguna Beach, California, to attend a sister's wedding.

"We were all so proud of him," Terry said, admitting how much she has learned about unconditional love from her relationship with her brother.

"There is always some good in what seems to be bad," she said. "Someone looking from above could see it."

Then Terry revealed an amazing insight. "I don't believe my brother has schizophrenia," she said. "I believe schizophrenia has my brother."

Terry Polnasek, a Wisconsin native, shares her struggle to understand how her brother Jeff changed her life and tells of his struggle to understand her.

The Advocate

Diane France of Albuquerque, New Mexico, is writing a book aimed to deliver a much-needed message: "Never, never shake a baby, no matter what."

"Often someone will shake a crying baby out of desperation. The child generally quiets down, but the reason is because there is a concussion," she said, beginning the story of how Patrick, a brain-injured child became her son.

One cold December evening in 1990, Diane slipped on the ice and sustained a head injury. Diane, a special education teacher, who worked for twenty years with learning-disabled and brain-damaged youth, was suddenly unable to work. Like her students, she struggled for two years to regain her memory and physical confidence.

"I couldn't subtract five from seven," she said. "There were times I felt suicidal."

Then something uplifting happened. At a whimsical lingerie party, Diane met twenty-three-year-old Sarah, a single mother, and her two-year-old son, Patrick. "I fell in love with that little boy with blonde hair and blue eyes," Diane said.

But while Sarah was at work one day, her boyfriend, who was taking care of Patrick, lost his temper and struck the child for not cooperating. Patrick flew across the bathroom, slamming headfirst into the cast-iron bathtub. He was unconscious. Then the man shook Patrick, trying to wake him.

According to the hospital reports, the shaking caused him to go blind. That Patrick had detached retinas is evidence of Shaken Baby Syndrome.

The limp child was rushed to the emergency room. Sarah came running. The young mother, who did not have a good relationship with her own mother, called Diane for help.

"I could feel what was happening with Patrick because of my own brain injury," Diane said. "And I could see that what happened was two lives were taken that night. Sarah was in complete shock."

For the next six months Diane stayed with mother and son at the hospital—leaving only to fight the court system that was going to release Sarah's boyfriend on simple bail. Like a Joan of Arc, Diane called in her army—judges, attorneys, and influential friends—demanding they put pressure on the court to raise the bail, thus keeping the man locked up.

They listened. The man received an eighteen-year prison sentence.

Diane, the advocate, fought the next battle on hospital ground. When Patrick was ready for home care, the social service department declared Sarah incapable of caring for her child. Patrick, now blind and quadriplegic, was to be placed in foster care, separating him from his mother.

Concerned, Diane persuaded the court to release them both to her care. The court agreed to do this—if Diane passed the inspection for foster care of a disabled child.

So Diane gathered her forces again, pulling together her family and community in a city-wide effort to convert her garage into a living quarters. Her grown children put up drywall, local businesses made sizable contributions, and Make-a-Wish Foundation donated the air conditioning.

It was a triumphant day when Sarah and Patrick with his feeding tube, suction machine, respiratory equipment, leg braces, and anticonvulsant medications came home.

For the next nine months, Diane jeopardized her own health to care for Patrick. Sarah, heartbroken and emotionally unable to care for him, stayed for just a few months, then said goodbye to the son she lost. Not long after that, Patrick was admitted to the hospital for breathing problems. This gave Diane time to realize that she couldn't manage Patrick's care by herself.

This time Patrick was discharged from the hospital to foster care.

"Maybe that wasn't so awful," Diane said looking back. "It gave Sarah a chance to reconnect. Foster care's philosophy is to work towards reuniting the child with the mother."

But after a year passed and Sarah was still not in the picture, Diane knew in her heart that she and Patrick were meant to be together. This time, Diane asked the sisters of Casa Angelica, a facility for severely handicapped children, for help.

"It was a long shot. There are rarely openings in a program where children are lifelong residents," Diane said. So when the sisters said yes to Patrick, Diane considered it a miracle—one that made it possible for her to adopt Patrick on February 26, 1996.

Though it's painful for Diane to tell the ongoing story of Patrick, she remains encouraged by her son's incremental recovery. Mother and son swim together, play baseball on Patrick's school team, and attend church on Sundays. Patrick can see shadows now, can stand with assistance, and is learning to communicate in short sounds.

"We work on speech, purposeful arm movements, range-of-motion exercises, and we laugh a lot," Diane said.

She also claims that Patrick hears and understands a lot more than he lets others know. Recently, he got *shushed* for making loud sounds in church.

"I guess he really wants to be heard," said Diane, praising the child who was once declared brain dead. "He's become a spoiled-rotten comedian with more potential than any of us professionals could ever imagine."

Diane sees the gift of Patrick is that he brings strength to the weak, laughter to the worried, hope to the defeated, and fear to the unknowing.

"When people visit Patrick thinking they are going to cheer him up, they are the ones who are cheered," Diane said.

Then she paused to say, "You know, the real advocate is God. He was there all the time and still is."

Decision to Have Child Brings Forth Togetherness

When Gary and Esther Flores learned that their unborn child had severe, life-limiting birth defects, they did much painful soul searching.

"There was a dead silence between us," Gary recalled. "The amniocentesis had reported the worst—trisomy 18, a genetic condition that would cause multiple birth defects —heart anomalies, cleft lip, and breathing problems. The female fetus had very little chance of surviving.

The family, already stretched to pay its bills, now faced the birth of a disabled child.

To make things worse, the couple, who live on the Hawaiian island of Oahu, knew that more than eighty percent of couples who suffer the death of a child eventually separate. It's the toughest adversity to endure.

"I thought we had no alternative but to have an abortion," Gary said.

Then he prayed. *God, I know I am supposed to give my burdens to you, but you have so much to worry about. I don't want to burden you, but I could use some help.*

Even without the pregnancy, their lives were not stress-free. There were stepfamily issues. Esther and Adam, her teenage son from a previous relationship, already felt estranged from the growing family. There were serious financial concerns. Gary, who works as a firefighter/paramedic for the Federal government, was facing a possible reduction in force (RIF) action and government shutdown that year. And there was the big question: Was it fair to ask the children—Adam, fifteen, Tobie, five, and Nicole, two—to experience the traumatic death of a sibling?

Agonizing over the decision, Esther sought help.

"My doctor said, 'It sounds as if deep down you don't think you are doing the right thing with abortion. I can't make the decision for you, but I can pray with you.'"

On Esther's lap were two scrapbooks full of pictures and a folder of handwritten messages from family and friends.

"I prayed that God would change Gary's mind about the abortion," Esther said. "I was afraid I would blame him later for the decision. We were already snapping at each other frequently."

Then son Adam cast his teenage vote. "You ought to have the baby. Give her a chance," he said.

Adam may have spoken, but the real decision had to be made by Esther and Gary. A few days later, while making arrangements at the mortuary for the cremation of their unborn child, they both changed their minds.

Neither knew what the other was thinking.

"I knew I couldn't live with the abortion," said Esther.

"Later that day, I heard Esther crying, so I went to her," Gary said. Then he revealed his new decision. "Let's keep the baby."

"Then a peace came over me," he said. "It was as if God was letting me know everything would be okay."

Although Gary and Esther knew the ordeal would press the whole family to the limit, they mustered the strength to go ahead with the pregnancy. Miraculously, their decision pulled them closer together.

"Adam even did a video interview of us as a part of a school project," boasted his mother.

Caitlyn Celeste was born on the Epiphany, January 6, the same day that Christians believe the three Wise Men brought gifts to the Christ child. The four-pound infant lay motionless on her mother's stomach for eleven long minutes. Then she cried, as if to say, "I'm alive, I made it!"

With the help of hospice, the family took their tiny bundle home for her final few weeks.

"That was the hardest," Esther admitted. "And it was a huge challenge for Gary. Trained as a paramedic to save lives, he promised Caitlyn that he would not try to revive her."

On March 3 Caitlyn died at home amid the family who loved her. The funeral was filled with neighbors, family, and friends who were touched by the courage of the Flores family. And the obstetric physicians who stood by Esther and Gary's decision made a special gift—there would be no charge for their services.

Looking back, Esther says she has learned to listen to her heart and not to take the easy way out. Gary says he is more empathic, especially with those he cares for as a paramedic. Both Esther and Gary feel the experience enhanced their marriage and family unit.

"We had a special gift," Esther said. "Many parents lose their children at birth. We had Caitlyn for nearly two months."

"It's only because God gave us the strength," Esther said. "In just the ordinary circumstances of our lives, we could have broken up before this."

Then a question just popped into my head. "Where did you two meet?"

Now a long way past those carefree days, Esther looked at Gary and laughed.

"We met in college in a child management class," she said.

Indianapolis Prays for Peace

As we drove into Indiana, all I could think about was finding the story we needed to finish our book. It had to fit into
the chapter, "Mixed Blessings." The next morning we found
the Reverend Les Galbraith—and our story.

A handyman hired to remodel a home in a residential
area was working late one night. When he started home,
someone stuck a gun in his car window and killed him.

At 7:00 A.M. the next morning, fifteen volunteers, the
police, and a cameraman gathered at the site of the crime.
Despite bitter cold, they joined hands, wept together, and
prayed for peace. Then Reverend Galbraith poured a few
drops of sacred oil in the form of a cross to reconsecrate the
ground. After the service, people lingered, sharing their
hopes that prayer would make a difference.

"A prayer service is a form of peace," said Galbraith,
the group's organizer, who believes Americans can no longer
run away from the violence in their cities. "We must take a
stand, express our sorrow, and begin the healing process."

The stand began a year ago when the people of Indianapolis asked the police to crack down on hard drug dealing. But the attempt to reduce the problem ignited two days
of street disturbances, resulting in broken store windows
and more than twenty arrests. The police brought out dogs
and told the people to stay indoors.

A number of pastors tried to calm the situation, but this wasn't enough. The Church Federation of Greater Indianapolis, an ecumenical body, met to brainstorm possible solutions.

"We wanted something positive to come out of this," said Galbraith, a tall, lean man in his fifties.

One minister had heard about a program in St. Louis, Missouri, where, after a homicide, people would gather at a church for a prayer service. The Indiana group decided to use this model but to take it one step farther. They would go to the site of the violent death within forty-eight hours and hold a service.

On February 14, 1996, the handyman was murdered, and the program was launched. "When the people in the neighborhood saw the police and the media, they came out of their houses. And when they found out what we were doing, they joined us," he said.

The group has reached as many as 240 participants. Galbraith says the services are sensitizing.

"Violence doesn't seem real to us because we hear, read, and see so much of it. Yet none of us knows when our life or the life of a loved one will end. We don't want to think about it," he said, wrinkling his brow. "We'd rather tune it out."

Today the list of volunteers includes hundreds. Yet another list is also mounting. Galbraith handed us the composite of this year's victims of violence: more than one hundred deaths so far.

"Often it's too soon after a death for the family to be at the immediate prayer service," said Galbraith, who attends them all. "So every three months we have a citywide 'Service of Remembrance and Peace Making.'"

They say the Lord's Prayer, light a candle of remembrance for each victim, and sing songs such as "We Shall Overcome." Later, the names are engraved on a peace pole so that those who died are not forgotten.

The families appreciate the services. Galbraith shared a story about a teenage boy who was accidentally shot and killed by his best friend, a neighbor. When Galbraith invited the mother of the deceased boy to the quarterly service, he didn't know she had not been able to go home since that fatal day. After the service, she told him, "The healing has begun, I can go home now."

Throughout the interview, we were moved by the number of times tears blinded Galbraith's eyes.

The next day, Galbraith called to tell us that a woman had been stabbed to death in her home on Drexel Street. He invited us to attend the service and gave us directions to her house.

We arrived at the service ten minutes late the next morning, having miscalculated the bustling morning traffic. We were apologetic, but Galbraith was unruffled.

"What's important is that you showed up," he said.

About ten of the volunteers were still sharing feelings. We spoke with several of them and were impressed with their dedication to the healing process.

"Violence shouldn't happen," Galbraith says. "But when it does, there is something we can do. We can show up. We can show we care."

Prisoners Put Right Foot Out

Doing the hokey-pokey helps children identify left from right. But what helps them distinguish between right and wrong in a world high on violence? In adult life there's no swift way to shake it all about. Crime is a serious matter.

"But an even greater crime might be continuing to condemn persons who really have turned their lives around," warns Ilona Lind, elementary school teacher and weekend volunteer at the women's correctional center in New Castle, Delaware.

We were ushered by a prison guard into the visitors' room at the Delores J. Baylor Correctional Institution for Women. The heavy metal door clanked and locked behind us. We sat at a table waiting to speak with Cindy and Brenda, two inmate volunteer coordinators for the Alternatives to Violence Project. Ilona had arranged for us to meet them to see for ourselves how the program is turning lives around.

The AVP program, designed by Quakers in 1975 and based on conflict-resolution skills, is grounded in the belief that there is a power for peace and good in everyone, something that reaches far beyond skill development. The AVP program is designed to build the foundation for community: self-esteem, mutual respect, caring communications, and creative problem solving. It also reaches into the realm of higher power.

Cindy, a cheerful, chestnut-haired woman in her thirties, was sitting across from us. She started to talk.

"The enrollment is by word of mouth. There has been so much interest over the two years that we can just barely keep up with the paperwork now," she said. "Forty-five percent of the inmates—that's about three hundred inmates—have participated in all three levels of the voluntary program."

The heartwarming outcome sustains Cindy's commitment. "When people complete the weekend program, they are tearful. They have achieved a family closeness, something many have never felt before," she said.

Glowing, she added, "The program helped me see who I really am inside."

Cindy plans to bring AVP into her community when she is released.

Then Brenda, a tall, dark-skinned woman with serious brown eyes, entered the room, greeted us, and began sharing her insights.

"What leads people here is anger. I discovered that I was one who kept a lot of anger inside," she said. "I just decided if I'm going to do time, I'm going to make it work and find out what was making me so angry. I was angry when I was a child."

Both Cindy and Brenda spoke of their improved communications within the prison and with their families on the outside.

"My daughter and I really talk now," Brenda said, touching her heart.

"I know there will be a lot of negative forces when I get out [of prison]," Brenda admitted, but she feels she has direction now. With her prison-learned computer skills, she can find a job. She plans to bring AVP into the schools.

"If kids have the tools—the skills that transform anger—they won't resort to violence," she said.

When the heavy door closed behind us, I thought I'd feel relieved to be on the other side. But I felt sad, as if leaving behind something of great beauty and wonder. That evening, Ilona shed some light on my apprehension.

"Though the AVP program is designed to be used with anyone, the contrast between doing the program with administrators and with prisoners is incredible. People who aren't in prison don't realize they put walls around themselves," she added. "People in prisons are more honest and easier to work with, more willing to change than people on the outside."

Since Ilona's work with prisoners, she has become increasingly concerned with a growing number of people who believe that former prisoners should be feared and shamed for the rest of their lives. Ironically, the AVP program covers the underlying causes of violence—fear, prejudice, false judgment, and stereotyping. Where's the hokey-pokey that can turn us all about?

For more information write to Ilona Lind, AVP Delaware, PO Box 196, Hockessin, DE 19707.

16

Family Matters

Family provides the basis for great joy, the foundation to love and be loved. But the downside has a depth equal to its height. The loss of family is the most crushing of all human blows.

Each family is endowed with its triumphs and failures. No two are alike, and no two are all that different. To know people who have worked hard to keep their families together, sometimes against all odds, is encouraging. To hear stories of what motivates those who reach out for lost members, fulfilling the dream to reunite, is inspiring.

Deep in the Heart of Texas

The world looked upside-down and backwards to Estes Turner, the way it looks to a newborn child. But he was forty-eight, married to a wonderful woman with two happy, healthy sons. He owned his own home in Cleveland Heights, Ohio, and his own business. Why did he feel so empty?

Estes and his wife Diane decided to try counseling. A few sessions made a big difference.

"We were so fortunate to have a therapist who identified that my adoption played a significant role in my relationship with my wife and my sons," Estes said.

Estes seemed to have been living in the dark. The therapist encouraged him to go to a support group meeting of the Adoption Network of Cleveland. There Estes began to remove what he described as, "the scrim—the last translucent barrier between the stage and the back wall in a theater." For Estes, there had always been something between him and the world, as if the world was happening out on the stage, and he was behind the scenes.

"At that first meeting, I realized there were lots of people wandering around in that same darkness," he said. "I discovered a relationship with people I did not have access to before."

At weekly meetings, he began examining the questions that had lain dormant since he was a young child growing

265

up in Texas: Who am I? Where did I come from? There is so much wondering that surrounds adoption.

"Eventually, most adoptees become disinterested because of the answers they get to their questions. By adolescence, other problems come up and the confusion and loss of vague identity all goes underground," he said. "In my case, the underground, secret life had some pretty devastating effects on how I related to the world."

As so many adoptees report, the pain began to surface after his adopted parents' death and at the birth of his first child. Though as he grew older, his adoptive mother encouraged him to start a search for his birth parents, but he feared betraying those he loved.

"I was so locked up about it. I was interested but couldn't take a step," he said.

Indeed, in 1946, when Estes was adopted, things were locked up. It was customary for parents relinquishing their child for adoption to sign an agreement forfeiting all rights including any contact or any involvement in their child's life forever.

"Most people were in such a vulnerable state when they signed that the agreement became an impenetrable oath, a hurdle too high to jump," he said.

More often the grown children who want a relationship take the first step. For Estes, the active search began after two-and-a-half years of support group preparation. Even then he took baby steps: a letter looking for records in Texas, a phone call leading to nowhere. Eventually, he hired a professional in Texas to look for information about birth registry that led to an important discovery. Estes was registered under his birth family's name, not his adopted parents' name. Using this information, he made more phone calls and wrote more letters but still made no connections.

"I knew I had to look deeper inside myself for the answers," he said. So he signed up for a personal growth workshop where he got in touch with a crippling belief.

"I had a story in my mind that kept me stuck. It was that my mother didn't want me. She didn't love me enough to keep me. If I actually found her, I would have to realize this as truth, not just a story I made up," he said.

Then a new thought peeked through. "What if my mother loved me so much that she was able to give me over to strangers out of her inability to raise me?" he said.

This thought, in context with how he feels today about his own children, birthed a new possibility. Estes' worldview was shifting. No longer was he like a newborn, upside-down. He was right-side-up, awake, and inspired.

As he began to believe this new story—one he was given as a child, but could not grasp—something deep inside posed even another question.

"How, then, can I withhold my love from this woman any longer? What if she dies, not knowing that I love her? By not making an all-out effort, I am doing to both of us something I cannot live with any longer!" he said.

Then the miracles began. "The world seemed to have realigned itself to match my new belief," he said. "We decided to take our family vacation in Texas where I was born. I knew I had to go back, to uncover the records myself."

Inexpensive airline tickets simply showed up. College friends in Texas offered their home. And the whole family arrived in Estes' hometown late in the day on August 9.

The next morning, the couple set out on an adventure. At the county courthouse, they discovered that the public is permitted access to birth records after fifty years. Estes, forty-eight, was stretching that day, like a two-year-old against a yardstick.

"But in the case of adoption, the original birth certificate is a legally sealed document that can never be released. But, remember, I knew my birth family name," he said with a twinkle in his eye.

"As if she were an angel, a woman appeared in the county clerk's office," he said. "She walked up to us and asked, 'What can I do to give you what you came here for?'"

The couple asked for the birth records and gave her the family name. Assuming they were relatives, she informed them the records were open in twenty-five years. Diane nudged her husband to break the spell of disbelief. Minutes later, the woman reappeared, holding the original birth certificate.

"We were frantically copying information, thinking any second she's going to catch on to us," Estes said, with a smile as wide as the state of Texas. With joyful, screaming eyes the couple looked at each other as if to say, 'Let's get out of here!'

"I felt as if we had robbed the bank," said Estes.

And surely, they had robbed the bank of time.

Outside the building, Estes stared at his birth mother's name.

"I felt strange, yet strong and positive about it," he said. "The missing pieces were all there—her social security number, her birthplace, and where she attended college."

So the couple locked arms and headed for the college where—behold, another angel appeared.

"For the first time, someone consciously wanted to help," Estes said. For the first time, he admitted that he and his wife were on an adoption search. The clerk smiled widely and revealed that she had done an adoption search in California. She flew toward the record room with abandon.

"By 6:30 P.M. we had my mother's address and phone number. She was listed as a resident in Kansas," Estes said.

This is the point where many adoptees stop. Not knowing how to make that call or how to manage possible rejection halts many searches. But Diane and Estes had rehearsed possible scenarios, intending to maintain a calm exterior in the face of wild excitement.

"I had written just what I wanted to say on a piece of paper," Estes said.

Miraculously, the connection was made on the first call. To the woman who answered to the name of Margaret, Estes said who he was and why he was calling. He gave his birth date, where he was born, and ended with a sentence designed to be as gentle as possible: "And as of today, after two years of active searching, my search has led me to you," he said.

There was silence.

Then out of the darkness he had known so well, the answer he yearned for came ringing through. "Yes." she said softly.

"I didn't ask if she was my mother," Estes said. "She just knew. I could tell she was very frightened. It was still a big secret. Her children didn't know. Only her husband knew."

The first conversation between mother and son was very brief. A time was set for their next phone meeting. "It wasn't like a big wonderful reunion at that point, but it was a beginning," he said.

Estes initiated the first calls and did most of the talking. Then there was a three-week silence.

"So I sent Margaret a greeting card and a picture of my family," Estes said. "That turned out to be quite significant because we look so much alike."

What happened next was a breakthrough. Margaret called her son! After forty-eight years of separation, she was reaching out for the child she never got to hold.

"All adopted children fantasize that their birth parents will come for them someday. It's more of a longing than a wish to be retrieved," said Estes. "I didn't know how much I wanted to be wanted until that call."

The process accelerated with more phone calls and letters. Then mother and son spontaneously decided to reunite on December 7, Estes' birthday.

By herself, Margaret flew from Kansas to Cleveland to be with the son she literally had never laid eyes on. Separated all those years, they would have to rely on their soul connection.

That evening, Diane, Estes, and Margaret sat on the Turner's living room couch and cried together. "My mother had lived a life of shame and secrecy. She had to start giving that up now because it just wouldn't hold in the face of so much love," Estes said with new confidence.

What Estes did not know was that when he began the search for his birth mother, she intuitively felt his call. She had been sitting in her living room in Kansas, watching a program on adoption when she spontaneously said aloud, "My son is looking for me."

Jeremiah's Influence

Before Jeremiah was born, Trina stole money from vending machines and hung out with her friends late at night. She was a street urchin and soon-to-be single mom. Her parents were divorced, and her mother's policy was "You can do whatever you want, just don't get caught."

"But some accidents are good," Trina said.

Trina, fourteen, met Frank, who was thirty-something, one warm summer night in July 1974. Frank, a handsome Mexican-American, called out to Trina from his car window and offered her a ride home. Trina told Frank she was a little older. Frank said he was a lot younger. They shared a beer and Trina, wondering what all her friends were bragging about, had sex for the first time.

The following spring, Jeremiah was born into a very confused household. One evening when Trina was walking to the grocery store to buy diapers, she met Frank again.

"Can you believe it? He drove by and asked me if I wanted a ride," she said.

That's how Frank learned that he had a one-year-old son. Skeptical, Frank drove Trina to her mother's home so that he could meet Jeremiah. The dark-haired, half-Mexican little boy was surely his. That evening, while walking with Trina around his favorite golf course, Frank cried tears of joy.

Trina's life continued to change. Working with her high school counselor, she became an emancipated minor. In the process, Trina received a scholarship to Outward Bound in Colorado, a program where she would rock climb, learn self-reliance, and a myriad of social skills. Jeremiah would stay for a month with his father.

"Outward Bound's motto is 'I can do anything,'" Trina said. "Well, when I returned to Kansas, there was a lot to be done."

While Trina was learning self-reliance, her mother moved out of town, abandoning Trina and Jeremiah. On her own, Trina found a job, rented an apartment, and became a responsible mother. Frank, however, drifted in and out of their lives. When he said he would pick Jeremiah up to take him to a birthday party, usually he didn't come. And when Trina refused to change Jeremiah's last name to Frank's, he left town.

Ten years later, Trina received a phone call from the prodigal father. Frank, forty-six, was dying of heart disease. The man who had spent most of his life playing golf was now asking for a relationship with his son.

Ironically, Trina was fourteen when she met Frank, and Jeremiah was fourteen when Frank resurfaced in their lives. Only God knew how long Frank would be around this time. His heart was beyond repair. His only hope, a heart transplant, probably wouldn't happen. But maybe he could mend the matters of the heart.

"We talked," said Trina. "Frank seemed sincere."

Frank became a committed and consistent parent. If he said he was going to take Jeremiah someplace, he did. For the first time, he bought his son clothes and participated in his school activities. Things went so well that by the end of the year, Jeremiah, now fifteen, moved in with his dad, two blocks from his mom.

Then Trina did something surprising. With compassion and forgiveness in her heart, she decided to marry Frank, making him eligible for better insurance and possibly a life-saving transplant.

"We were parenting our child, and we had become a kind of family," she said. But Jeremiah had mixed feelings about it. "He was afraid we might be doing something illegal," said Trina, aware that she had raised her son to be mindful of the law.

The couple married but kept separate living arrangements and led separate lives.

All did not go well, however. One Saturday morning, Frank lost his temper and hit Jeremiah for not getting up to mow the lawn. The sixteen-year-old, who had never been treated poorly, withdrew and moved back to his mother's home.

"Frank was on a lot of medication, and I could see that he was dying right before our eyes," Trina said, recalling how Frank had cried when they talked.

A few days later, Jeremiah saw his dad driving down the street. They made plans to go to a baseball game later that week. Returning home, Jeremiah announced, "It's all going to work out fine with Dad. We can have a good relationship. I just can't live with him"

But Frank died a few days later.

When Trina and Jeremiah arrived at the hospital, the hallway was crowded. Trina, standing guard between Frank's noisy family and the room where Frank lay dead, encouraged Jeremiah to spend a few moments with his father.

The lavish Mexican-Catholic funeral was spiced with controversy. Was Frank's body to be cremated, ashes spewed as he wished over the first tee at his favorite golf course? Or was his mother going to see that nice big casket sink into the ground where she could keep an eternal eye on her son?

"It was midnight when we held hands and prayed over Frank's ashes on the first tee," said Trina, shaking her head. Frank's sister was trying to console her sobbing mother. Frank's girlfriend was complaining, and Frank's brother passed around the box of ashes, inviting everyone to "say their peace."

Jeremiah scooped up a bit of his dad's dust, tossed the remains to the Kansas wind, and said, "My dad and I had some disagreements. But all dads and sons have fights. I know you love me, Dad, and I love you."

Trina, who was telling us the story while we sipped coffee in a Wichita cafe, just smiled.

"You have to remember, I had a lot of mixed feelings about this guy," she said.

Alan's Quest for Healing

There are many ways we find our stories. Friends and acquaintances give us names of ordinary heroes they know. People who read about our journey across America offer their own heartwarming stories. And sometimes one lead leads to another. That's how we met Alan Christianson.

June Wortman, our friend from Cleveland Heights, Ohio, suggested we call Betty Foley when we arrived in Phoenix, Arizona. June met Betty during World War II. For several years, they were prisoners in an internment camp in the Philippine Islands.

We talked to Betty and were understandably impressed. Betty's story is one of forgiveness. She holds no grudges; she identifies war as the only enemy, and she doesn't focus on the past. After our interview, Betty, a gracious woman with pure white hair, gave us our next lead.

"The one you really want to interview is Alan Christianson. He's engaged to my granddaughter," Betty said. "Now there's a story!"

The next day we sat in Alan's living room, sipping herbal tea and listening.

"All my life I've had this deep interest in healing, nutrition, and the study of different cultures," he said.

When Alan was in his final weeks of nursing school in Minnesota, he learned of his acceptance to Southwest

276

Naturopathic Medical School in Phoenix—a program that combines Eastern and Western medical philosophies.

"I didn't have the financial resources to back me," he said—not with a frown but a smile. "But a voice said, 'Tell them yes. You will go.'"

That same day the soon-to-be-medical student received a phone call from his adoptive parents. Good news. The house they had struggled to sell for the last ten years sold that very day. They could help with his medical school tuition.

Although a holistic medical school would satisfy Alan's yearning for diverse knowledge, it didn't fully answer his inner quest. The diligent student took another step, one that brought him face-to-face with the mysterious stirrings inside him.

With the blessing of the parents who raised him, Alan began the process to find his biological mother.

In December 1992, Alan contacted the agency where his parents adopted him. The social service liaison was quick to locate his birth mother. Alan first met her over the phone, finally learning the circumstances that surrounded his birth twenty-four years earlier.

"Linda was just seventeen when she left Denver and went to Minnesota to have me," Alan told us. She never told Alan's father that she bore his son. She had no more children.

Seven months later, in July 1993, Alan met his biological mother. "She was tearful and truly happy to have me as a part of her life," said Alan, recalling their first embrace.

That fall, Linda visited Alan in Phoenix where he was attending medical school. That's when she revealed his father's name was David Frawley, and that she knew him as a teen in Denver. Linda provided the information Alan needed and her blessing—to find his biological father.

"I went to the Denver phone book and called the two men with that name. Neither had attended high school in Denver, so I knew it was not either of them," he concluded.

Then Alan followed another lead, one that rose from deep inside. He had heard that the last name his mother gave him was the name of a familiar Eastern medicine author. Frawley had written *The Yoga of Herbs* and other books that Alan had read. The man was an expert in the field of Ayurvedic medicine. Could it be his father?

Wild hope flashed like lightning through his open mind. But then the fear of disappointment and possible rejection thundered it shut. What if this accomplished man wanted nothing to do with him?

For the next two years, Alan's studies took precedence. To think about finding his father was just too scary. Then one day he got the courage. "If this man is on a spiritual path, then he will understand my letter," Alan said.

David called the day he received Alan's letter.

"He was able to say, 'Yes,' he had dated Linda and, 'Yes,' he must be my father!" said Alan. "David also had no other children and was happy I found him."

Then David shared something strange. A week before he had received Alan's letter he had an astrological reading. He was told that if he were to have had a child, the time would have been 1967-68. That's the year Alan was born!

David sent airline tickets to Alan and his fiancée Kirin so that they could come to meet him. "I just kept looking at him, thinking, 'Are you really my father?'"

Alan said, "It was wonderful."

In March 1996, Alan and Kirin were married in Sedona, Arizona. All four of Alan's parents attended the joyous family occasion.

Father's Day Message

In 1978 Bruce, photojournalist for this book, found him-self in a difficult situation. After nine years of marriage, his wife, Mickey, was leaving him and their three children. She decided she just didn't want to be married.

Ruthie, a foster child since birth, was nine years old. Joshua, who was already adopted, was five years old. And Jesse, who had not been officially adopted yet, was a lively two-year-old.

The adoption agencies encouraged Bruce to consider backing out. Raising three African-American children as a single parent was something they didn't recommend. And there was a heated controversy in the 1970s about white parents adopting African-American children.

Bruce, who had fathered all three children from baby-hood, knew that keeping them was the right thing to do. Ruthie and Josh were tightly bonded. They had already ac-cepted Jesse as their little brother. Besides, the children knew no other father. Bruce was determined that he and the chil-dren would learn how to live without Mickey. They would stick together.

Both the agency in St. Louis, Missouri, where Bruce and Mickey got Ruthie and the agency in Erie, Pennsylvania, from which Jesse was being adopted, challenged Bruce's ability to be a single parent. But after proving that he could provide the children with food, clothing, medical coverage, shelter, educational opportunities, and lots of love, Bruce was allowed to continue, alone, as their father.

Oddly, Mickey faded into the past, with not even a trail of Christmas cards.

Why did Bruce fight to keep his family together? "We were a family. I couldn't break that up," he said.

As a toddler Ruthie used to ride on Bruce's shoulders. She was full of energy, giggles, and smiles. Her strong will and outgoing personality were perfectly matched. "I couldn't kill her spirit by abandoning her," Bruce said.

Joshua was already adopted. When he was an infant, he had braces on both legs to correct a severe bowing. He never complained. He was a caring, sensitive child whose easygoing attitude held them all together. "We were truly bonded. I couldn't abandon him," said Bruce.

And Jesse was charming; anybody who ever got near him liked him. He went to bed happy and woke up happy. For some reason, Jesse had been turned down for adoption by another family. "I couldn't turn him away too," said Bruce.

So the Madsens piled out of their huge Victorian home that Bruce had renovated on Cherry Street in Erie, Pennsylvania, and moved to a small rental house outside of town. There they licked their wounds and learned how to live as a single-parent family.

It wasn't easy. But Bruce, an industrial engineer whose hobby was time management, developed a rugged routine, squeezing the corporate demands of General Electric, where he worked as a project manager, with the demands of a growing family.

He would rise early, shower, and get ready for work before waking the children. While the children were dressing, he made breakfast for all of them. With hats, coats, mittens, boots, and books, they piled into a yellow Volkswagen Beetle and headed for their first stop, a daycare home where Jesse stayed. Next, Bruce delivered Joshua and Ruthie to the school bus stop. Then he would drive thirty miles to work. After school, Josh and Ruthie walked to the daycare home to stay with Jesse until 6:00 P.M. when Bruce would fetch them.

After dinner and homework, Bruce lined them up for baths and tucked them all in by nine o'clock. "I'd sit in the hallway between their rooms and read bedtime stories. Then we all went to sleep," he said.

As the children got older, the schedule got bigger. There were baseball practices, ice skating lessons, and class plays. Bruce hadn't a minute to himself. But there were humorous times that still make the Madsens smile—such as the day Bruce discovered that he had four kids, not three.

"I was in the living room when I heard a huge crash in the kitchen. The glass gallon milk container had shattered. Milk puddled on the floor and splashed onto the kitchen walls," Bruce recalled.

"Who did this?" he demanded. All three children stood as if statues planted in the mess, wide-eyed and dead silent. Then, amazingly in unison, they said, "Not me."

From then on Not Me, the invisible kid, was responsible for most every problem, from missing pie to broken windows.

Bruce Madsen and his son Joshua

Like all parents, Bruce wonders if he did a good job parenting. Certainly, there were times when things could have gone smoother. That's why a Father's Day greeting from Joshua, now twenty-six, means so much to Bruce. Luckily, we captured it on our phone message machine.

"How ya' doin' Dad?" said Joshua, who is a paramedic for the city of Cleveland. "Out of everybody and out of all the circumstances I could have come across, God really looked out for me, man, because he blessed me with you. This was on the strength, man, on the strength. He blessed me. He put me with you."

"I got to tell you I love you more than I love anybody in the world. You have done more for me, and I love you more than anybody. I need to tell you this every day, but I don't. I'm telling you today. I guess Father's Day is as good a time as any. Happy Father's Day, Dad. You're the best."

Joshua's Family

"Guess what," was the beginning of another great voice mail message left by Joshua, twenty-six. Deep inside, Bruce knew that his 6-foot-4-inch, muscular son whose body is housed in an ancient soul, had found his way home—had located his birth mother.

In January Bruce was cleaning out some old file folders when he came across something he didn't know he had—two pages of adoption information about Josh from 1972. To be uncovering the past felt so right, although it also felt strange.

As his three adopted children grew older, Bruce encouraged them to search for their birth families if they wanted to. Josh casually filed that information somewhere in the back of his mind. However, when the folder bearing the names of his birth mother, Grace Harris, and his sister, Carol, was serendipitously uncovered, his interest turned a cosmic corner.

Bruce, wanting the best for his son and inspired by Estes Turner's story, "Deep in the Heart of Texas," mailed the information to Josh, including a brochure about the Adoption Network of Cleveland, a support group that helps adoptees work through the reunification process.

On Father's Day 1998, Josh took Bruce to Jacobs Field to see the Cleveland Indians clobber the New York Yankees. It was a great day. While enjoying hot dogs with Stadium mustard and tall glasses of draft beer, Bruce casually asked Josh if he had thought any more about finding Grace Harris. He had but was stymied about getting started.

That evening Bruce offered to help Josh go through the information and think through the process. Leslie, Josh's girlfriend and dispatcher for a paramedic team, made a few phone calls and found a Carol Harris in Painesville, Ohio.

The next day Josh called a friend and co-worker, Veronica, who lives in Painesville. Wow! He felt as if he'd won the Wheel of Fortune. Veronica filled in the blanks solving the puzzle. Indeed, she had graduated from high school with Carol Harris and yes, her mother's name is Grace. The bonus was that Veronica's mother, Johnny May, is friends with Grace. They all attend the same church.

The next day Veronica and Johnny May arranged for Grace to meet Josh. They told her, "There is a young man who wants to meet you. Someone from twenty-six years ago."

"When I met Grace, I didn't tell her who I was. I just made her acquaintance," Josh told us. "The next morning I called her and told her gently that I had something to read to her."

Josh read the paper Bruce had sent in January regarding Grace Harris and the circumstances surrounding her decision to give her son up for adoption. First of all, she wasn't married. Second, she was already struggling financially to raise her daughter. Finally, she wanted her son to have a better life than what she thought she could offer him. Slowly, Grace recalled the past but then quickly moved into the present.

"Well, where are you now?" she asked. "When can you come to see me? How soon can you get here?"

Later that day, Josh met Grace and his Aunt Judy at the home of Grace's mother. Grace took her newfound son into her mother's kitchen and announced, "Ma, there's somebody you have to meet, your grandson."

The older woman gazed at the handsome paramedic who works for the city of Cleveland. She moved her glasses up as if to focus better and when the tears welled up in her eyes, she said, 'Well, come give your grandma a big hug.'"

Before long, more relatives—cousins, aunts, and uncles—pulled into the driveway to meet their new family member. "Everybody was hugging and kissing and crying," Josh told us.

They all gathered around the kitchen table, shuffling through years of family photos and telling stories.

Josh is the youngest of five children. Ronnie, the oldest, is musical like Josh. His maternal grandparents raised him. Unfortunately, the grandfather is deceased. Ronnie is married and lives in Warrensville Heights, a Cleveland suburb. Grace raised Carol. Like Josh, she had braces on her legs when she was young. She is married and has a child. Brian and Gary were raised together in a foster home. Four years ago they reunited with Grace.

That weekend the Harris family threw a big picnic so that everyone could meet Josh.

"It was a beautiful day," said Josh, over his next voice mail message. "Call me, Dad."

17

Can-Do Attitudes

*D*etermination comes from a strange and wonder-ful inner strength coupled with a nondescript staying power. It's the energy that guides and directs countless community projects. Sometimes determi-nation is heavenly inspired. Sometimes it's a matter of team spirit. More often than not, the motivation is an individual's decision simply never to quit.

Oh, Chute!

While sipping iced tea and catching up with our Ohio family, we happened upon a story that my sister-in-law Diane was embarrassed to admit but couldn't help telling.

When Ron and Diane Schumaker of Cuyahoga Falls, Ohio, committed themselves to becoming homeowners, they had no idea what that would entail, nor the risk they were putting their marriage under.

One day, Diane, so happy to be doing the laundry in her own home without the need for a fistful of quarters, made a discovery. The towels and dirty socks she had tossed casually down the clothes chute weren't reaching the wooden laundry box in the basement.

"I did notice that I was really low on underwear," she told us, trying not to laugh. This was a serious matter.

Obviously, the laundry was stuck in the chute between floors. Being a risk-taker, she dropped a heavy lead crystal vase down the small opening located in the second floor bathroom. "It wasn't a prized possession, and it would land on top of the laundry and push the clothes through," she thought.

The vase never made a sound.

To protect the vase, Diane sent a few more clothes down the dark hole, fattening it up for what she was beginning to think was a new sport: laundry bowling. Down went several pairs of Ron's socks and a fluffy bath towel. Now she could try something heavier. Surely, that was the answer to the clogged artery. More push, more power.

With intention, she tossed down a heavier and certainly meaner object, a large red brick. She meant business. Reflecting on this phase of the laundry Olympics she told us, "I wish I had put more force behind it."

With the cunning of a wildcat, her eyes searched the basement for better tools. She spied a four-foot piece of piping. Surely, this was the answer. "I bent it with all my might to get it into the angle of the chute," she said. "Then I duct-taped a tree branch on it to give me full extension. I had this problem licked!"

Like Wiley Coyote in yet another attempt to outsmart the tireless Road Runner, Diane raised her mighty lance and took a stab. The clothes didn't budge, but her arm was beginning to hurt from overextension.

Next, the determined homeowner duct-taped a hook to a pole, thinking she would fish out the blockage, piece by piece. She caught nothing.

That evening when Ron got home, he tried his hand at the stubborn laundry canal. He created his own rig. Diane stood in the background, thinking that her piping apparatus had a better chance, but she didn't dare tell her husband, who was getting piping angry.

"Ron had to step away from it. He was getting so frustrated," she said.

For the next two days, the new homeowners took a break from household concerns. Maybe the problem would solve itself up by some act of God. An earthquake might help.

Friday night Ron went out with some friends, leaving Diane behind. But that's what she wanted. She would take a crack at the laundry Olympics again. Spirit renewed, the challenge was on. First she tried the vacuum sweeper extension. No luck. Then she called the fire department and asked for advice. No suggestions. Finally, she called a co-worker who offered a swimming pool pole.

"I didn't want more stuff caught in the chute, so I said, 'No thanks.'"

The next day Diane called Mr. Fix-it, a friend who is always willing to tackle home projects. Fix-it does carpentry work and mends what's broken. Although Diane's spirit wasn't broken, her mind was on tilt, and she was beginning to admit she needed outside help. "But it isn't an emergency," she told him with pride. "Come at your leisure."

Eight months later, Fix-it showed up with a full support team—his wife and his large shepherd dog named Hobbs. When all his high-tech gizmos failed, he cut a hole in the wall close to the clog and pushed with all his might. Diane, Ron, and the Fix-it team stood at the bottom of the chute like a cross-country coaching team, cheering each item across the finish line: an old crystal candy dish, a bottle of Victoria's Secret body lotion, a long-forgotten pair of silky pink pajamas, and the mighty red brick.

Not wanting to risk falling into the trap of another clothes clog, the homeowners made a lifesaving decision to board up the chute forever. After all, they'd done without it for eight months!

Parish Priest Works Wonders

When the auctioneer wanted an opening bid of five thousand dollars for a 1987 school bus, Father Emilian Swiatecki's head was reeling, but not his heart. Dressed in black with a white collar, the priest thrust his auction card in the air and shouted, "Fifteen hundred dollars!"

"It was my lucky day," he said. "We got our bus."

Every Tuesday after school, more than sixty children climb into Father Swiatecki's white-painted bus and head for St. Joseph the Worker Catholic Church in Moore Haven, Florida, where they attend religion classes. The fifty steps from the bus to the church are filled with joyful noise. Then there is silence. At the entrance to the old Spanish church, the children bow their heads and then scramble into assigned pews, their makeshift classroom.

The ageless priest with thick dark hair stands before his young parishioners. A single *shush* gains their attention.

"Children, you are here to be prepared for life," he says, in echoing staccato. "You are the future."

Father Swiatecki is a powerful visionary. When he reached retirement age in 1990, he asked to be sent to some forgotten area that needed help. That's how the Polish-born priest landed in a small migrant-laden community on the western shore of Lake Okeechobee. He hasn't had a moment's rest since.

When he arrived, there were just a dozen parishioners, mostly migrant workers, a cement block church that hadn't been painted in thirty-six years, and several acres of overgrown land.

Just as in the movie, *Field of Dreams*, Father Swiatecki took a chainsaw and cleared several acres of land.

"This was a swamp," he said, gesturing to what is today the best soccer field in five counties. Last year, St. Joseph the Worker's team won the regional soccer trophy.

But the real goal was reached when the police reported to the parish priest that youth crime in Moore Haven is down, thanks to his efforts. "They're too tired to get into trouble," the priest said.

But it hasn't been all fun and games. From December 1991 to June 1996, the priest, like the poor he helps, lived in deplorable conditions—a small trailer located fifty yards from noisy Highway 27. The overworked man got very little rest. Six months into his new assignment, he was admitted to the hospital in Orlando for triple bypass heart surgery. Two weeks later, like Mother Teresa of Calcutta, he sprang back to cut the grass and continue his projects.

Behind the new rectory Father Swiatecki built this year and beyond the ball field is a medium-security correctional facility operated by Wackenhut Corporation. A few years ago, the priest persuaded the prison builders to install a larger sewage treatment facility than what they needed.

"The city of Moore Haven can tie into it so that we can get more businesses to come here. This means more jobs," he said.

But his main concern is the new changes in immigration law. As of April 1, 1997, those who have not started the paper work to become permanent residents are being deported. And those who have lived here longer and have not paid income tax have to pay their back taxes.

"The people come to me asking what they should do. I tell them they must learn English and the American culture. They must become citizens; otherwise, they will be like slaves," he said.

Recently, the priest hired a lawyer to help the Spanish-speaking people to get their paper work in order. Then he paused to fill in the other side of the equation. "Without the migrant workers, citrus and sugar cane farmers will have huge problems. There are 473,000 acres of sugar cane to harvest. The people are willing to work hard for low pay. Most Americans won't do that," he said.

Father Swiatecki's next step is to build the much-needed parish hall.

"I will have classrooms for the people to prepare for citizenship," he said.

The man in his early seventies has a running start: plenty of land, volunteer teachers, and a congregation that has multiplied like loaves and fishes. What began with twelve families now has grown to 120 Spanish-speaking and ninety English-speaking families.

From the rectory window, we could see the kids reboarding the white bus.

"If I get all the young people behind me, we'll change the face of Moore Haven," the priest said. "I just need those classrooms."

Then with a sparkle in his eye, he said, "Listen, I could do it for $150,000. I'm just waiting for a guardian angel to help us."

Sacramento Senior Gleaners

In 1808 Spanish Captain Gabriel Moraga sailed up "the big" river—one he later named the Sacramento. Hanging over the clear blue waters were live oak and cottonwood branches draped with wild grapes, elderberry, and black-berry vines.

"Es como el Sagrado Sacramento!" he exclaimed, which translates to, "This is like the Holy Sacrament." He saw Sacramento as a Garden of Eden, a blessed land.

Today, the Senior Gleaners, a group of volunteers 1,850 strong, still hold this image of Sacramento as the land of plenty. And for nearly twenty years, they have proven it.

In 1976 a handful of senior citizens decided it was un-conscionable that people in their community were going hungry when there was such an abundance of food left in the fields of Central California. The food must be gleaned, not wasted, and the poor must be fed is their credo.

A band of thirty senior citizens began picking the fruit in their own backyards and distributing it to local soup kitch-ens.

Next, they got permission from farmers to pick and gather the food left to rot in orchards and fields. That is how the nonprofit organization grew. More and more vol-unteers joined the cause, and local grocery stores pitched in their leftovers.

The Senior Gleaners are the major all-volunteer food distribution agency for Sacramento and the adjoining counties, providing 230,000 meals per month to ninety-five charities that feed the hungry.

Gleaning isn't a newfangled technology; it's an old biblical practice: *"When you reap the harvest of your land, you shall not be so thorough that you reap the field to its very edge, nor shall you glean the stray ears of grain."* (Leviticus 19:9) In summary, leave food for the poor.

Bob McMahon, a Navy veteran and volunteer, escorted us on a private tour through the administration building.

"Meet Kay Greyson, our fundraiser," he said, gesturing one hand out as if to say, "Ta-dah!" We poked our heads into an office to say hello to a neatly dressed, silver-haired woman who swiveled around in her chair to greet us.

"And I had no previous experience either!" she said, boasting what's so for many volunteers who have learned new skills—busting the myth about old dogs and new tricks.

In the warehouse, forklifts are lifting, delivery trucks are loading, well-oiled conveyor belts are rolling, and a multitude of salvageable food in boxes and cans is being sorted, all by volunteers.

"We have to pay four dollars a month to work here," joked Pat Conyers, a Gleaner for ten years. Pat and Robert Conyers glean the orchards and fields in the Sacramento Valley whenever the agency gets a call from a long list of participating farmers.

At 6:00 A.M. the Conyers meet their crew of thirty, who carpool to sites around Sacramento. This week they will gather walnuts. What they get in return is fellowship, a boost of self-esteem, and the satisfaction that comes from helping others.

"It's good for the heart to work here too,"chimed in a spunky, flowery-shirted woman who overheard our conversation as she was zipping by.

"As you can see, the volunteers are worth a fortune," said McMahon, referring to the "can-do" attitude, the camaraderie, and the enormous amount of work that's done Monday through Saturday.

"The average age here is seventy-three," he said with a huge smile, shattering more myths about older workers.

We gathered lots of "good vibes" as we went from room to room. McMahon introduced us to carpenters using table saws, men carrying cartons into walk-in freezers, a group of women knitting gifts for convalescent homes, a round table of letter-stuffers addressing the latest newsletter, and the talkative kitchen crew preparing lunch.

All major food stores in Sacramento participate, so as long as there are human errors—a bottle of strawberry preserves with a grape jelly cap, slightly dented cans, crackers in a slightly smashed cardboard box, there will be enough food.

Just one hour with the Senior Gleaners changed my way of thinking, too. What could be saved? What could be given away? What could be stretched or used more efficiently? What if abundance is paradoxically more a function of being thrifty, and gleaning is the way to celebrate what we already have versus consume, consume, consume?

The holiness of gleaning must have rubbed off. *Voila, Sacramento!*

The Senior Gleaners, 1,850 volunteers strong, at work in Sacramento.

Our Lady of the Rockies

The late afternoon sun was aglow on the Montana mountains as we rode into Butte. Inspired by the white luminous
statue high on a peak overlooking the copper mining town,
we sensed that something special was evolving here.

Historically, the people of Butte have suffered tragic
losses, common in mining communities over time. But working together, the community has transformed its mining mis-
fortunes into lasting treasures—with help from above, they
say.

In 1979 Bob O'Bill promised to build a statue of the
Virgin Mary and put it in a public place if his wife Joyce
recovered from a major illness. She did.

Bob, now challenged to keep his promise, envisioned a
four-foot statue of Mary. When he shared his plan with
fellow workers, they said, "Let's think bigger." Together
they conceived and committed themselves to a ninety-foot
statue to be christened "Our Lady of the Rockies," a tribute
to all women, especially mothers, to be placed, somehow,
atop the Continental Divide. It took five years to complete.

We met with Bill Bermingham, AKA "Mr. Positive," current director of Our Lady of the Rockies nonprofit project.
Bermingham retired in 1979 from Montana Bell, where he
taught the art of positive thinking and how to use visualization to manifest desirable outcomes.

"This is the best example of visualization I've ever seen. Belief comes first, evidence later," he said with a twinkle in his eye.

Early in the project, Bermingham donated his time to the project, teaching the principles of positive thinking to four thousand citywide participants.

"Butte was a sad city in 1979. Everything had stopped," he said. "More than a thousand miners were on the brink of losing their jobs. The mining industry was in financial distress, and the people needed something to boost morale."

The people of Butte, rich in mining and engineering skills, carved a switchback road up a mountain. With donations of manpower, money, land, and equipment, they saw to the sculpting of a ninety-foot steel statue to be named Our Lady of the Rockies.

Then they enlisted the Nevada Air National Guard and the U.S. Army Reserves from Butte, along with a civilian team, to complete the job. On December 20, 1985, the statue was lowered in four parts by helicopter—all fifty-one tons of steel slipped onto a four-hundred-ton concrete base.

"Women in the grocery stores left their carts. None of us did anything but pray that day," said Nancy McLaughlin, owner of a pasty shop that fed meat pies to the men during the four-day assemblage.

"Since the Lady was put up there, things have turned around," Bermingham said.

In miner's lingo, *Fire in the hole* means the dynamite has been lit. The completion of this insurmountable project fired the hearts of Butte citizens for more recovery projects.

In 1994 Gerry Walter, a gray-haired VISTA volunteer, researched the Butte historical archives for information about the 1917 mining disaster that had claimed 168 miners' lives.

A committee was appointed to raise money for a monument to them, but the great flu epidemic of 1918 wiped out most of the community. When would these miners ever be honored?

"As I was reading about these young men, something took place in my heart, and I knew this was a story that must be told. Men trapped in the mine shaft had written farewell letters. They knew they were going to die," Walter said.

Exactly seventy-nine years after the disaster, on June 8, 1995, Walter and eighty-five others gathered to launch another Butte community project. Overlooking Granite Mountain Mine where the 168 men died is the beginning of a commemorative wall. Before the snow flies (and in Montana, that's early), the grid will be laid for custom-engraved bricks.

A woman from Texas who grew up in Butte at the time of the disaster expressed her gratitude. "There was never closure to my father's death," she said.

"You don't have to have a relative who died in a mining accident to participate," Gerry Walter said. After all, she doesn't.

She does, however, have something equally as powerful: a belief that the immigrant pioneers must be remembered for their strength and honored for their contribution to Butte.

*Our Lady of the Rockies, a tribute to all women,
stands atop the Continental Divide, watching over
Butte, Montana.*

It was a cold and rainy day when the bagpipes played
"Amazing Grace" and Walter gave her dedication speech.

"Something inside just took over, and I wept when I
said, 'You are standing on hallowed ground,'" she said.

As we stood on the foundation of bricks and looked
across the valley, we could see, over the headframe of the
mine, Our Lady of the Rockies.

It was a vision of Butte we won't forget.

They Came, They Liked, They Stayed

The great Northwest is oversized and awesome—a wild land where there is little amnesty for error except for the rough and tough attitude of the people who come to live there. And those who, by some twist of fate, move to Alaska say it has to do with freedom, opportunity, and the spirit of adventure.

In Tok, Alaska—where there is scant snow but the temperature drops to sixty below zero—we met Roger Skarie, Vietnam vet who loves living in the forty-ninth state. After the war, Skarie got a government loan to start a small business, a bakery shop. "I paid it off and have been in business for fifteen years," he told us, placing his thumbs into the armholes of his apron and pulling them out.

"Things are good here. This is how it works. Every tenth barrel of oil goes to the state. The state invests the money. Then a percentage of the interest, like a dividend, is returned to the people. This year it amounts to about $1,500 for each Alaskan." For Skarie that's big bucks because he can't feed four boys on doughnuts alone.

In Valdez we met Larry Hodges, current owner of the Hook Line and Sinker and former engineer for General Electric. "I used to smoke a pipe, wear a suit everyday, keep my hair cut, and go to the right parties," he told us shaking his head.

More than twenty years ago, Larry moved from Michigan to Alaska. He finds it easier to endure the Alaskan winters with the 110-mile-an-hour winds, frequent earthquakes, and heavy snow than the politics of corporate America.

Halfway from Fairbanks (home of the International Ice Sculpting competition held in March) to Denali National Park (home of Mount McKinley, the highest mountain in North America at 20,320 feet) is the tiny town of Nenana. There we met Jane G. Haigh, museum curator and author of *Gold Rush Women*, a collection of short stories acknowledging the pioneer women who, a century ago, followed their men on foot over the 3,700-foot Chilkoot Pass. They wore heavy skirts, layered petticoats, and warm jackets and carried backbreaking packs and lofty dreams en route to "opportunities" in the frontier North. "These are the forgotten women who turned a wilderness of brawling gold camps into a decent land of schools and churches and homes," she told us.

With similar determination, Jane came to Alaska following the lead of her older sister. And though her sister has moved on to easier paths, Jane, a tireless trekker, has held on. Currently, Haigh is a candidate for the state senate, running on a pro-subsistence ballot. Jane believes that the native people should be allowed to fish and hunt freely on the land.

In Homer, at the southwest tip of the Kenai Peninsula, we spoke with Sharon Bushell, who came to Alaska with a girlfriend to work in Talkeetna for a summer, met her husband, and stayed.

Sharon doesn't miss the rush, the crowds, and the lines of traffic, characteristic of where she came from, Washington state. As a matter of fact, she has had the time and space to pursue her dream of becoming a writer. She has a biography service—something that began fifteen years ago when she wrote her father's life story from a series of audio tapes and short interviews. "I'm so glad I did," she told us. "Six months after I completed the project, he died unexpectedly. When I read those stories, mainly in his own words, it's as if he's in the room with me."

For ten glorious days, we drove our 1984 Dodge Ram camper van on and off the ferry boat, making our way through the Inner Passage: leaving from Haines, then on to Sitka, then Juneau, and finally, Ketchican.

Haines has a fascinating history. The town was founded in 1881 as the site of Fort Seward, an Army fort. During World War II, it became a training camp for recruits. After the war, the loss of troops threatened to devastate Haine's economy. But that didn't happen because five veterans and their families purchased the Fort's eighty-five surplus buildings, making it their home. Ultimately, the college-educated Easterners, whom everyone doubted could survive the rugged Northwest, were key to the preservation of the Alaskan arts and instrumental in launching the Marine Highway System.

At the Alaska State Museum in Juneau, Kai Augustine, museum guide, gave us a helping hand. When we discovered that we were out of cash, Kai insisted that we be his guests. Since he was originally from Hawaii, we asked Kai how he came to live in Alaska. "Since I was seven, I wanted

At the Alaska State Museum in Juneau, Alaska,
Bruce and Julie learn about the native culture from
30-year teacher Kai Augustine.

to go to Alaska," he said. He related a tale about an old
Eskimo woman who at the age of fourteen was kidnapped
by a harpooner who sailed the Bering Sea. They married,
had three children, and came to live near Kai's family in
Maui. She told many tales of life in Alaska. Eventually, Kai
became a teacher so that he could teach in various parts of
Alaska. This is what he did for thirty years.

18

Out of the Ashes

To be willing to look at the past and all its difficulties with an open mind and an open heart requires courage. To forgive and forget, treating all persons with kindness, is wisdom. To be grateful for all of life's twists and turns, while making the most out of what you have been given, is faith in action.

Thus, out of loss, a new life can emerge.

Albert White Hat, Sr., a Lakota Sioux

There are no billboards and no businesses in south central
South Dakota, only a few lonely farms and a small cemetery, protected by a fence, keeping cattle out and reverence in.

Near the Rosebud Reservation a row of black-eyed
Susans lines the way into the town of Mission, home of
Sinte Gleska University, where Lakota Sioux can study education, social work, and business while learning the ways of
their ancestors.

There in a log cabin we met Albert White Hat, Sr., a
teacher of Lakota language skills.

According to White Hat, people come to the reservation seeking medicine men who, they think, can give them
answers that will take them down a path to greatness. "We
have no such path," he said. "We believe in hard work. In
our philosophy, we don't seek power. Power is a gift you
can't get through a vision, quest, or a sun dance."

In 1961 White Hat had moved to Cleveland, Ohio, as a
part of the assimilation program set up by the U.S. government to mainstream Indians into the white culture. In the
industrial Midwest, he learned about noisy machine work
and smelly factories. He also met two men who changed
the course of his life.

In a local bar, he told a stranger how he loathed factory work. "When the day is done, there is no relationship with those you work with side by side," he said. "I couldn't live like that. It's too scary. The whistle blows, and you don't know these people anymore."

Then White Hat told the man about Rosebud, highlighting his childhood when alcohol was illegal on reservations and life was better. "You are describing a beautiful place. I think you should go home," the man said.

While pondering this, White Hat talked to a co-worker. "He was intelligent and sincere, a DP (displaced person) who was seeking citizenship in the U.S.," said White Hat. "He told me he had been in the U.S. for ten years, and according to factory standards, 'If your brother is drowning and he has insurance, you are crazy if you don't help him drown.'" These words, screaming of twisted values, echoed in White Hat's mind for several years.

"Because of what these two men said, I knew I would go home someday," he said.

Ten years later, White Hat returned. "I went back to be with my older brother who had lost his wife," he said. "I knew that I had to face the reservation problems that were now more complex: alcoholism, diabetes, and heart disease."

The biggest step back, however, was when White Hat faced his own alcoholism. "A friend told me about a thirty-day treatment program, and I went," he said.

But getting sober has its own problems. Sobriety isolated White Hat from those he loved. When he became sober, his friends shunned him—a stab in the heart that nearly broke him—except for the help of a parish priest in the nearby town of St. Francis. White Hat rented a room from the priest and drove an ambulance as his work. But he worked among troubled people.

"The alcohol problem on the reservation was one hundred percent. People were getting physically sick now. Many were dying from cirrhosis," he said.

For the next three years, White Hat worked and lived in St. Francis. In 1974 when he began studying the Lakota language, something clicked inside him. "Language is the heartbeat of the culture," he said, touching his chest. "When the language is destroyed, so, too, are the people."

Coached by a linguist and a social worker, the determined student studied to become a language teacher. When he learned about lesson plans, a new world opened to him.

"All my life I had been conditioned to be dependent on the reservation system," he said, describing a dependency as deadly as alcohol. "Now, for the first time, I could conceptualize what planning ahead really meant."

He also learned how his older brother had grasped planning ahead before him. In 1949 White Hat's brother had planted a seed by starting locally run schools. By the late 1960s, the seed had germinated into a college movement. Within a few years, classes were offered on the reservation. In 1979 White Hat's brother died, but not his dream.

When the school's final accreditation for the two-year, associate degree program was up for renewal in 1982, White Hat, now the chairman of the board, and several others went to Chicago to meet with the officials. And, because White Hat doesn't believe in easy paths, what happened next was the result of hard work and curriculum excellence.

"The officials asked us to come into the meeting room for the decision," he said, describing the tense moment. They had good news. "Our curriculum qualified as a four-year, baccalaureate degree program."

Then White Hat told us a story. "In my language, there is no word for *animal*. Everything belongs to a nation," he said.

One day, a friend told White Hat to come quickly and look at the canyon in his backyard. It was covered with birds, all hawks, an incredible sight.

"You're lucky if you witness the gathering of a nation in your lifetime," he said. "The hawks were coming together to renew their relationships. That my people could be like those hawks is my greatest wish."

And that may happen.

When White Hat was a child, speaking Lakota was not encouraged and there was no written language. Today, he and a committee of experts are developing the phonetics of the ancient language so that the sounds and rhythms of the past can renew the lost spirit of the Lakota Sioux.

White Hat's book, *Reading and Writing the Lakota Language,* was published in 1998 by the University of Utah Press. He is confident that it will help his people reunite as the hawks did.

Siena/Francis House

Out of the ashes of drug and alcohol abuse, Paul Koch came to the Siena/Francis House in Omaha in 1988, needing more than a shelter and a good meal. He needed a new life.

"My association with the homeless gave my life meaning," Paul said. "I remember at one point hollering out in total frustration, 'I just want to make a contribution.'"

Paul's cry in the darkness was heard. Today, he is the executive director of the Siena/Francis House that assists homeless people who are drug and alcohol abusers.

We were sitting in his office admiring the creative decor —12 feet of taped-together white paper highlighted by red and blue marking pens, the product of brainstorming. Bold, black arrows pointed to prioritized tasks. It is virtually a wall-to-wall version of the shelter's five-year strategic plan.

Paul, a short-statured man with tall ideals, leaned back in his swivel chair, locked his hands behind his head with elbows out, and shared his story.

"I said what most substance abusers say: 'It will never get me.' Well, it did get me," he said, punctuating his words and scratching his beard. "It ruined my life. I woke up sleeping on the floor of a warehouse, thinking, 'Gosh, this isn't how I was raised. This isn't who I am.'"

In high school on Long Island, Paul wanted to join the Peace Corps. Instead, he enlisted in the U.S. Air Force. He

311

was stationed in Nebraska and sent to Vietnam. After the war, he returned to Nebraska, chose a career in business, bought a house in the suburbs, and complained that his life was empty—fertile ground for depression and substance abuse.

After completing a ninety-day treatment program for drug and alcohol abuse at the Siena/Francis House, Paul got a job driving a cab. He called a friend and boasted about taking action about his problems. But beneath his pride was a jittery cry for help. He was struggling, one day at a time, to stay sober.

"My friend knew that cab driving didn't support sobriety. It was too soon to be on the street. He offered to help me get a job at the Siena/Francis House as the volunteer coordinator," Paul said. "My first response was to say I didn't want to go back there."

But it felt right. And since treatment, Paul was in touch with his feelings. So he applied for the job and got it. At midlife, he was coming full circle. It wasn't the Peace Corps, but it was community service.

Paul's enthusiasm for his new job was contagious. Soon he was asked to be interim director while the board searched to fill the newly vacant executive director's position. Again, friends urged him to apply for the job.

"They could see something in me that I couldn't see in myself. I didn't think I was qualified," he said.

However, having *been there* is a special kind of qualification. And though Paul looks round and jovial like Friar Tuck, his friends knew that in his passion for recovery, Paul moves swiftly like Michael the Archangel, defending the homeless with his mighty sword.

Just nine months into his sobriety, Paul became the executive director, chosen not for his ability with books and numbers, but for his compassion and dedication to helping people.

"I would not have had the confidence to accept without my newfound faith in God and the support of my wife and friends," he told us. "Working here has been the most rewarding eight years of my life."

As we slipped through a long winding corridor, accompanied by the sounds of pots and pans clanging in the kitchen, Paul stressed the importance of treatment programs and Twelve Step groups.

"Food, shelter, and clothing are just Band-Aids," he said, "Eighty percent of the residents are chronic substance abusers. That's hard-core work. The staff is constantly dealing with relapse, recovery, and spirituality. The treatment goals are independent living and making a contribution to others."

As we said goodbye, Paul rattled off the names of other shelter directors he thought we'd like to meet.

"Go see Baloney Joe in Seattle and Clancy at the Midnight Mission in Los Angeles," he said. "You'll love their stories!"

"Yeah, You Rite!"

The day Jo Ann's husband Donald committed suicide was the worst day of her forty-six years of life. Some people never recover from such trauma.

But in a four-year process, Jo Ann turned a tragic loss into a passionate cause by writing a book on how to survive widowhood through humor and simple kindness.

Jo Ann Rosenfeld read about our two-year adventure in the *Times-Picayune* in New Orleans and called, offering to show us around the city that she loves. Raised by Italian parents and six doting uncles, Jo Ann married her college sweetheart, Donald Rosenfeld, twenty-three years ago, adding Jewish heritage to her already warm Southern ways.

Jo Ann greeted us at her front door. Dressed in cool cotton clothes and wearing walking shoes, she was ready to go. We hugged at first sight. Then she handed us a gift box full of New Orleans-style red beans and rice, Cajun and Creole cooking spices, and several mouth-watering cinnamon buns.

"These are things you just have to have," she said with Louisiana pride.

Six years ago, when Donald shot himself because of overwhelming financial pressures, Jo Ann had to find some things to hold on to—the love of her home, New Orleans; her

314

cultural roots; her teenagers, Jamie and Jesse, and her God-given sense of humor.

"I made a decision," she said, describing a vital part of her grief process. "I could either be cynical or spiritual. We have to help one another, and we have to laugh more."

This is what her book *Yeah, You Rite!* is all about. To top it off, she became a stand-up comedian.

"These are streetcars, not trolleys," Jo Ann instructed as she drove us down live oak-lined St. Charles Avenue.

"There's Dominican College and Loyola Law School. Notice, about every third block there's a church or a synagogue. Tulane University, Audubon Park, and the Zoo are all great places to learn the history of New Orleans," she said, as we continued toward the French Quarter.

At Cafe Maspero, we devoured oyster and shrimp po-boy sandwiches on real French bread. Then we strolled down Royal Street—stopping to enjoy a street musician playing "Danny Boy"—and peered through antique shop windows, admiring pricey seventeenth-century knickknacks.

Sitting under the awning at Cafe du Monde, we watched other tourists walk between the Mississippi River and Jackson Square while we sipped *cafe au lait*, nibbled on fancy powdered sugar donuts called *beignets*, and became friends with our hostess from the Deep South. Jo Ann and Donald were married for many good years. They had the best of two strong ethnic backgrounds. What happened?

In her book *Yeah, You Rite!* Jo Ann devotes a chapter, "In Defense of Men," addressing this question. She speculates that Donald might be alive today if he hadn't had to face stigmas about loss of work that haunt men in our culture.

"When men fail at work, they feel that all is lost," she said.

Jo Ann acknowledges the men in her life and encourages less male-bashing.

"We must learn to recognize and acknowledge, the 'good guys,'" she writes. "You know them by their simple kindness."

"It is written in the Talmud that kindness is the highest form of wisdom," Jo Ann said. Recently, she was inducted into the Kiwanis Club, where she heard a story that demonstrates this wisdom. In 1930 during the Depression, a young boy without a father needed an operation. His mother was so poor she didn't have the means to get him to the hospital. Then Kiwanis stepped in. A Kiwanis Club member came to their door the next morning to take them to the hospital. As the child climbed into the man's car, he asked, "Mister, are you God?" The volunteer answered, "No, I am not."

The child persisted. "Mister, do you work for God?"

"No, son, why do you ask?"

"Because last night my mama asked God for someone to take me to the hospital."

By this time, we were at Audubon Park, where stately, two-hundred-year-old live oaks with lumbering branches swoop to the ground. Telling the story was difficult for Jo Ann. Her eyes welled up, and her throat began to tighten. Why? Because her heart is open—through a decision she made to be spiritual, not cynical.

The Green's Life-Giving Decision

You may recall the story of Maggie and Reg Green, whose son Nicholas was killed in September 1994 while the family was vacationing in Italy. We visited the Greens at their home in Bodega Bay, California, to do a follow-up story.

In October 1994, while the Greens were traveling in Italy, seven-year-old Nicholas was sleeping in the back seat of their rental car when a bandit's bullet pierced through the night, stealing the child's life.

The whole world cried, then gasped in awe when Maggie and Reg, without hesitation, donated Nicholas' organs to seven Italians.

"We thought it was very important to give his future to those who had lost theirs," Reg said. "We expected it to be a private decision."

But as soon as Maggie, Reg, and four-year-old Eleanor returned to their hotel, the media descended, capturing the dark side of tragedy, illuminated by the seven gifts of life. All of Italy threw its arms around the Greens.

"Nicholas struck a spark of love in the hearts of millions of parents and children around the world," said Reg.

Back at home in northern California, British-born Reg, who publishes a mutual-fund newsletter from his home office, launched a crusade. For three years, he and Maggie crisscrossed the United States and Europe spreading the news about the importance of organ donation.

"I am determined that as long as there is an interest, I'll do this work," he said.

We sat in the Green's living room, our eyes filled with tears, listening to a father's response. Maggie, who was picking up Eleanor at school, was due home any minute. A part of me wanted to meet this incredible woman who had lost her son. Another part winced at the thought of her pain.

Then she appeared, a tall, gracious woman in her mid-thirties with short, dark hair and sad eyes. Eleanor, like all little girls after a busy day, was cranky. She needed her mommy and daddy, not strangers in her house. We knew we should leave.

I made my notes and put the file away. But I couldn't get the Greens out of my mind or my heart.

Several months later, something miraculous happened. While watching the nightly news, my eyes lit up when I saw Maggie and Reg on national TV holding their newborn twins, Laura and Martin. I leaped from our tiny kitchen, rocking the rig and leaving the spaghetti sauce I was cooking. I bounced into the bedroom about fifteen feet away and hugged Bruce, who was at work on the computer, all the while shouting, "Thank you, God."

In October we received an update from the Greens. The people of Italy donated 120 bells that were sculpted into a Children's Bell Tower. The eighteen-foot work of art, mounted by the sea at Bodega Bay, was dedicated to Nicholas on October 27, 1996.

"It's a place where any parent can come for solace or inspiration, a place where parents will want to put their arms around their children or hold each other's hands," wrote Reg.

I imagine the twins and their big sister Eleanor standing beneath the sculpture. With rosy faces facing the ocean breeze, they are mesmerized by the music of the chimes, their brother's eternal song.

Finding a Christmas Miracle
in Humble Surroundings

One night the desert winds whipped through California's Soledad Canyon, howling and stirring up memories of winter in Ohio. Homesick, I crawled into the bed of our red pickup while Bruce held the flashlight. In search of a box filled with Christmas stuff that had bumped along with us since last April, I dug among the rubble and raised the dusty package with broken cardboard flaps from the cold metal floor. Cradling the box like a small infant, we brought the precious cargo into our warm home-on-wheels and placed it on the counter to be opened.

With delight we unpacked the contents: several toy wooden soldiers, ten sterling silver snowflake ornaments, two strings of red lights, two red wool scarves, two hand-painted Mexican doves, and a stack of holy cards tucked in a snippet of wrapping paper held by golden elastic string.

Although the holiday storybook I thought was packed in that square cardboard box was missing, the comfort of Christmas memorabilia made trailer living with no room for a tree—bearable.

In the morning, the very Christmas story I sought emerged in an interview with an ordinary hero living in the California town of Visalia, outside Fresno.

Like the little drummer boy, Mardy Friedman followed the star, though she had no gifts of gold, frankincense, or myrrh. And like the child who played his drum for the new-born King, Mardy offered her talents by tapping into the hearts of immigrant children with gifts of tutoring, mentoring, and multicultural studies.

"I don't go to church, but I'm very spiritual," said Mardy welcoming us at her front door. Her home—a modest one-bedroom dwelling decked with boughs of holly, angels on a high dresser, a trimmed California pine, a crystal manger scene, and a multitude of children's art —heralds *It's Christmas.*

"Christmas is in your heart. That's what I tell the children who come here. I think it's good for them to know about American traditions," said the woman, who was born Jewish and raised as an only child.

At age twenty-four, when she was in college studying to become an English teacher, Mardy had a stroke that crippled her left arm and leg. The stroke, caused by a congenital problem, changed the course of her life.

"I always wanted to be a teacher," she said. "And though I finally finished my B.A. in English, becoming a teacher never worked out."

Only years later, when she received a voucher for low-income housing that landed her in a neighborhood full of kids, did Mardy begin to see how her life might turn about, beginning right in her own front yard.

In 1992, carrying a book under one arm and a milk crate under the other, the disabled woman hobbled to the shade of a tree, stationed herself on the crate, and started to read aloud.

"I just saw a need," she said. "These children are transplanted from a Southeast Asian culture, where there is little written language, to California, where there is already a great mix of cultures."

And as she wished, a Southeast Asian child from the housing complex came to listen. More children joined each day. When the weather cooled, they moved the makeshift classroom into her house.

"The children called it "The Mardy House," and it stuck," she said.

There is no staff and no board of directors—just Mardy and anyone who wants to volunteer. Sometimes the older students help. Often the Kiwanis Club donates time and tickets to the cause. Mardy even has the Visalia police department participating in the after-school project that goes all year long. Last week, she arranged for twenty-five girls to see *The Snow Queen,* aided by the use of a D.A.R.E. bus. In March, the boys will get their turn.

The after-school curriculum includes arts and crafts for kindergarten through junior high. Occasionally, a high school student drops in to check it out. This week, the children, assisted by the high school Key Club, sold $300 worth of handmade gifts in front of Wal-Mart. Their first holiday bazaar was a grand success.

"The children work in 102-degree weather all summer long, making crafts to earn the money that pays for the neighborhood holiday party," Mardy said.

Where does this grateful woman with a disability and a meager income get the energy to keep The Mardy House open six days a week, accommodating a dozen kids at once?

Mardy Friedman launched an afterschool program for kids and found life's purpose.

"Thank you, God, for these kids," she said.

Recently, Mardy began volunteering at the Adult School, teaching English as a second language and citizenship classes. "Some of the parents of my kids are in the classes," she said.

Just Say Yes

When somebody notices that something needs to be done and says yes to getting that something to happen, the world works better. We call that making a difference. But it's not simple. Making a difference means more than saying no to violence, poverty, and injustice. It means taking risks, giving help, working in community, and saying yes to life, yes to love. Best of all, making a difference doesn't have to be a big deal.

Battery-Operated Bible Turns People On

"There he is again!" I shouted.

We were stopped at a busy intersection in St. Petersburg, Florida, when I spied "that guy," shouldering a cross —a seven-foot wooden monstrosity gliding on two rubber wheels.

We had seen him several days ago. That time he was walking along a bicycle path, and we were barreling, rig and all, down narrow U.S. Route 1 towards Key West.

Bruce reassured me, "If we are meant to interview him, we'll see him again."

"What's the chance of seeing a tall, slender man carrying a cross ever, let alone twice?" I groaned.

Then—boom. There he was, hundreds of miles later. This time we stopped.

"This is an Easter story," I said, jumping out of the pickup at the traffic light. My notebook and pen grasped in one hand, I waved furiously at the strange man with the other. As I flew across the street, I knew something more than a story was moving me. I felt such joy. The childhood tune *"Boom, boom, ain't it great to be crazy?"* danced wildly in my head.

The cross-bearing man, dressed casually in a T-shirt and khaki trousers, greeted me with, "Ain't it great to be crazy for the Lord?"

A series of chills shivered down my spine as I started babbling about our journey of hope across America. "And I suspect you have a few good stories to tell, like why you're carrying a cross, cross-country," I said.

Joel Gass, twenty-five, is fueled with high octane spirit. He quit his job as a youth pastor in Pensacola, Florida, on the last day of December to walk his talk and "heighten Christians' awareness."

Inside his homemade cross he totes a rolled-up tent, toothbrush, change of clothes, ("wear a pair, carry a pair"), and a Sony tape recorder. He walks about sixteen miles a day. In the evening, he pitches his tent on a church lawn, then rises early to carry the cross again.

"The cross is a symbol of death or surrender into a more spiritual life," he said.

We were shouting joyfully over the blaring traffic and the flap, flap, flapping of our clothes in the wind. It was over eighty degrees, and the Florida sun beat down on our heads like tiger's breath.

"Are you sure this isn't penance?" I asked.

"That's the point. Christians get too comfortable pew sitting," he said. "When the *Titanic* sank, the ones who really cared reached out and pulled in others that weren't safe."

By simply walking, Joel pulls people in. They stop, some out of curiosity, others to share their pain and shortcomings. A few make a commitment to lead a better life.

"One lady stopped her car and came over crying. She was depressed and didn't know why," Joel said. "She said she realized when she saw me that what was missing in her life was God."

Joel says God provides for him through people. "People buy me lunch. I found twenty dollars that someone put under a rock on the bicycle path," he said. "That was like the story of Saint Peter needing money to pay taxes."

"I vaguely recall that story," I confessed.

"Christ told Peter to look in the mouth of the fish—for a coin," Joel said.

Then he pulled a pocket-sized computer out of his backpack, punched in Matthew 17:27, and the biblical passage flashed onto the tiny screen.

"Whoa, what is that?" I asked.

He laughed. "If I pull out this high-tech, battery-operated Bible, people get excited. They want to hold it. But if I reach for the book version, they step back," he said.

While we were there, a man in a blue pickup stopped to talk. He said he admired Joel's courage. Then he shared his pain about being separated from his three-year-old daughter.

Next, a teenager on in-line skates stopped. After a short conversation, Joel pulled off his sunglasses and handed them to the squinting pilgrim.

I like Joel's open-air church with no pews to get stuck in. I especially like the simplicity of the roadside confessional—"Bless me, pastor, for I have forgotten to rely on God." And I like an America where a man can push a seven-foot cross along public roads without apologies.

Joe's Cardboard Ministry

Thanks for giving is this story's festive, November theme —thanks to a company in Indiana, a TV station in Kentucky, and a volunteer who never quits.

Six evenings a week, after his regular job at LexMark in Lexington, Kentucky, Joe Rice drives his twenty-foot truck to two main stops, the Casual Living Patio Center and Sears Delivery Services. At each stop, he backs up the white 1983 Chevy box to the loading dock, leaps onto the cement landing, and begins cutting the refrigerator-sized boxes set aside for him to recycle.

The proceeds go to his church. Since July 1994, he has donated $21,000.

Last summer, while helping Joe fold and pile high a load of cardboard, we learned how this recycling project started. Several years ago, his parents began recycling aluminum cans.

"They were going to give the money to my kids," Joe said. "But my kids didn't need it. So we gave it to a church member, Judy Harrison, a single mother with five adopted and eight foster children, all with special needs."

That's how Joe got the recycling bug. The first week he gathered a thousand pounds of the corrugated stuff, and sixteen weeks later he collected his first $1,000. The going price for cardboard fluctuates from a measly twenty dollars a ton to a whopping one hundred dollars for the same work. To date, Joe has collected over 880,000 pounds.

The money benefits Trinity Baptist Church in many forms—a needed ice machine, choir robes, a duplicating machine for the mission house, and money to subsidize the Wednesday night family dinner.

"Many people couldn't come unless the meal was free," Joe said.

What keeps this forty-eight-year-old all fired up? "The Lord is the one who keeps me going," he said.

"But how do you get time off?" we asked, knowing he hadn't taken a vacation in several years.

"Well, that's not easy," he said, stopping to scratch his head and take a deep breath. "Me and my wife want to go to Hawaii next summer for our twenty-fifth wedding anniversary, and I'm concerned about finding someone who can take over for ten days."

This recycling task is not like fetching someone's mail. It's a commitment that left undone could cost Joe the sought-after route. He didn't seem to be the kind of person who asks for help. So when we said goodbye to the tall, slender man, we secretly wished that we could somehow be of assistance.

A few months later, Bob Haverstick from Computer Business Services, a computer company in Sheridan, Indiana, called asking how his company could help. He had read about our upbeat news project in the *Indianapolis Star.* We told Bob about Joe's cardboard ministry, and he offered Joe $300 to hire someone to work the three-hour route.

Then we called the Reverend Doug Martin, engaging Joe's church community in a scheme with WKYT-TV to surprise him with the check.

*Hillary Wicai, formerly
a reporter for
WKYT-TV Lexington, KY,
promotes good news.*

*Joe Rice of Lexington, Kentucky, recycles
cardboard and donates all the money he
receives to charity.*

"It wasn't easy," said Sherry Prewitt, church secretary, who made many calls. "I had to tell Joe that the pastor really needed to see him at 2:00 P.M. Joe said he'd see what he could do."

Then Sherry called TV news reporter Hillary Wicai, who herself had requested the surprise two o'clock coverage. But Hillary had bad news. The phone system in Lexington had gone haywire due to a computer glitch, and she was pulled from the good news story and reassigned to cover the telephone problem.

Then Sherry saw Joe cutting cardboard in the church yard. He was waiting to see the pastor. "Joe mentioned that he took four hours off work to be here," Sherry said. "So I called Hillary back and told her. She apologized many times, but still she couldn't cover the story."

Behind the scenes, the secretly gathering church group was about to present Joe with the check when an unplanned surprise happened. Hillary and her TV crew hurried in with their cameras, creatively claiming that they were there to cover the telephone story.

Joe, still in the dark as to why the minister had summoned him, waited patiently in the shadows. When the cameras and lights were all set, Pastor Martin motioned for Joe to come forward—completely surprising the man who gives endless hours to others. With the check, the cardboard ministry would continue while Joe and his wife celebrate twenty-five years of love together.

With tears of gratitude, Joe thanked them all.

Hats Off to Nellie Gold

In 1961, after paying her rent and buying food, Nellie Gold didn't have enough money to buy her children presents for Christmas. When she saw the sadness in their eyes, she vowed never again to have a Christmas without gifts.

Today, Nellie directs the food ministry at a homeless center in Indianapolis. "I believe we are all just a paycheck away from being homeless," she said.

Sunlight beamed through a prism in the window of Nellie's office at the Dayspring Center and cast a rainbow on her shoulder as she spoke.

"I was living in Chicago. My marriage had failed. I was just getting by," Nellie said. "That spring, with seven dollars in my pocket and seven kids piled in an old car, I moved back to Indiana where my father had lived."

Determined to find a better life, Nellie found day work, eventually got a job with RCA, remarried, and for the next fifteen years worked hard raising her kids.

"But when I turned fifty-five, I lost three important men in my life—my husband, my brother, and my son. I decided to take early retirement," she said

After six months of washing walls and painting woodwork, the restless retiree began looking around. She noticed a school across the street. "The children were always fighting when they cut through my yard. So I started refereeing," she said. "I believe that love is the answer."

Then, with a little milk and cookies to sweeten the deal, she started an after-school Bible class. And when she heard about a soup kitchen opening in their part of town, she took seven boys to the dinner.

"I was feeding them anyway," she said.

The boys followed the manners Nellie taught them, swept the floors, and washed the tables after they ate. The cook was so impressed that she asked Nellie if she wanted a volunteer job.

"It broke my heart to see what was being served. It wasn't fit for dogs—no seasoning, no taste," Nellie said. She decided to help out.

When Nellie made her Southern-style corn bread with brown beans stewed in shoulder bone and sliced-up onions, the street people swarmed around.

"It got so they only came if I was cooking," she said.

Knowing that she, too, would need help, Nellie reached into her past. "People have not because they ask not," said Nellie, recalling the words of her minister-father. She began asking for better food from supermarket warehouses and meat markets. She also asked for funding. Confronting one influential politician, she said, "You're always hollering you can help—well, I need help."

But Nellie cooked through many stages and phases before help arrived. She recalls carting her table, her slow-cooker, and a tent to Kroger's parking lot while the men slept in various temporary places. "They never missed a meal," she said.

Finally, the funding came through and the food ministry expanded to include a homeless shelter for families,
thanks to Nellie and a few concerned citizens who raised
over one million dollars for the renovation of an old Epis-
copal church. Classrooms were turned into bedrooms and
a large office space became the home of a Head Start Program.

When the building was finished, they moved in. "What
a glorious day that was. I had an industrial-sized kitchen
and a walk-in freezer," she said.

Best of all, now there was a safe haven for families in
crisis, old men with canes, and young mothers with newborn infants. What began as a modest soup kitchen became
a four-hundred-meals-a-day food ministry and fourteen-
room shelter for families in crisis.

Nellie, a tall, handsome woman wearing a bright red
dress, walked us around the building, introducing us to the
Dayspring staff. We stopped to read the handwritten message painted in bold letters on the dining room walls:

*YOU ARE OUR GUESTS. WE EXPECT DIGNITY,
PRIDE, AND RESPECT. WE WILL NOT TOLERATE VUL-
GAR LANGUAGE. MEN, HATS OFF.*

Nellie, her children, and a band of angel volunteers will
serve between four hundred and five hundred Christmas
dinners this year.

"And we make sure that each guest receives three or
four gifts too," she said, recalling how in 1961 she didn't
have money to buy Christmas presents.

Then she paused to reflect upon all the years she's been
cooking at the Dayspring Center. "In 1983 seven boys
brought me here. I was working love on them. They worked
love on me," she said.

The Strength of Keeping a Promise

Most people don't make promises. Making commitments is just too difficult in a throw-away world. And besides, if you don't keep the promise, you're strapped with guilty feelings and risky resentment. It's not worth it.

Not so for Lin Miller of Fairview Park, Ohio.

In November 1994 Lin's former college roommate, Cathy Mauser, was diagnosed with advanced breast cancer. Lin was there when Cathy got the bad news. The doctors would try to save her, but the prognosis was grim.

"I made a pledge to her, in my heart, that I would take care of her, see her through this, whatever that would mean and whatever that would take," said Lin.

Lin, a registered nurse who works for Reminger & Reminger in Cleveland, arranged her busy work schedule so that she could stay with Cathy throughout surgery and also take her friend for her chemotherapy and radiation treatments. For a while, the treatment appeared to be working. Cathy, a counselor, was even able to see clients on a limited basis again.

Then, on July 14, 1995, Lin was out for a sunset sail, alone, on Lake Erie, in her sailboat *Spirit*. The marine forecast reported clear weather. But out of nowhere, a mean storm came roaring across the water. Ninety-mile-an-hour winds brought spitting hail, crackling lightning and giant, thrusting waves. Lin was thrown from her boat. The tiny vessel capsized, sank briefly, and reappeared far from her reach. Then it tumbled side-over-side in the distance and was gone.

"I thought I was a goner, too," she said.

Miraculously, two young men in a boat appeared. Despite zero visibility, they somehow spotted Lin's flailing arms and bobbing head. Like angels of mercy, they reached out and pulled her aboard.

"All three of us were screaming in terror," Lin said.

For the next hour-and-a-half, all three hugged the heaving boat and rode out the storm. When the Coast Guard rescued them, Lin was in shock.

"The scary part was not that I could be dying, but I had to face the question, 'Why had I lived?'" she said.

Six weeks later, as a part of her recovery from the trauma, she bought herself a new, bigger sailboat, a Hobie Cat with two hulls, a main sail, and a jib. She named it *Spirit II*.

"I felt as if I had a new life," she said. "Cathy was improving, and I felt so alive."

But in January 1996, Cathy, who just turned forty, began feeling ill again. Each week she needed more help. So Lin, who was beginning to feel drained, decided it would be best to move Cathy to her apartment for convenience. She could keep a more vigilant eye on her there.

"That's when I realized that I had been pulled from the lake to take care of Cathy," Lin said.

Cathy's condition continued to worsen. However, in March, Lin and her sister were able to take Cathy for one last trip to the Adirondacks. "Cathy loved the mountains.

It was her dream to be able to go there again," said Lin.

The end came in October.

The last night Lin sat up with Cathy she knew her friend was dying. She called Cathy's friends so that they could come and say goodbye. "I held Cathy in my arms until she took her last breath," Lin said.

Six months later, Lin wrote to us. "I'm feeling better with each passing week. Caring for Cathy was so intense. Then it all ended abruptly, leaving a big, black void. Sometimes the tears come uncontrollably. I'm still trying to get some kind of life back."

From the two-year experience, Lin learned to pay less attention to the dishes and more attention to what's really important—for the gift of one's self is the greatest to give. Best of all, she kept her promise.

"I saw Cathy through to the end. It may be the best accomplishment of my life," she said.

Lin thinks her life was spared so that she could take care of Cathy. I suspect it also had something to do with making and keeping a promise to a dying friend.

Raspberry Delight

Dotted roads on state maps indicate scenic routes. But all the roads in Utah are scenic. Our home-on-wheels climbed higher and higher into the mountains, following the white water of the Logan River. The top edges of these mountains look like stegosaurus backs, with pine trees running along their spines.

As we descended into the lush valley that defines Garden City, I spied a handful of people crouching and bending to pick berries in patches below. Then we saw a sign advertising what Garden City is famous for—FRESH RASPBERRY MILKSHAKES.

There was no way through this town without stopping. So over the river and through the last bit of woods we proceeded, to Grandma's Pantry on West Logan Road.

Before the truck had fully stopped, I jumped out and marched to the restaurant porch. Three steps later, I was through the door. My decision was made. "I'll have a raspberry yogurt milkshake," I announced to the high school girl wearing a raspberry print apron. Bruce asked for a raspberry yogurt cone.

We sat on the porch, sipping and licking pure pleasure. Plump red berries and cool chunks of frozen yogurt slid down our throats like kids on sleds. Then an old woman with white curly hair and grey-blue eyes and wearing a floral print dress stopped at our table and touched my arm.

"I've come all the way from Ogden [Utah] to get some of those fresh baked goods, and they are all sold out," she said with a made-up frown.

We exchanged smiles. Then she pointed her cane toward her friend who was waiting for her in the parking lot. "We came all the way for my ninety-sixth birthday," she said.

Noticing raspberry stains on her lips, I asked, "Did you at least get your fill of raspberries?"

"Oh, yes, my dear," she said.

We chatted about the beautiful day and the wonders of life, while my milkshake melted and Bruce's cone slumped. It just didn't matter. When she said goodbye, we stood by the porch watching her every step. Then I recalled the words from a sermon we once heard at the little Community Church in Sierra City, California.

By their fruits you will know them. The fruits are love, peace, patience, kindness, gentleness, generosity, faithfulness, and self-control. When these fruits are present, we know that spirit is present. Do we leave people feeling uplifted or drained and downhearted?

We were left filled with pure joy.

Epilogue

In 1995 when Bruce and I quit our high-paying jobs, sold our fancy house, bought a twenty-six-foot travel trailer, and headed for places unknown, we weren't just *Lost in America*. We were guided by something far greater than impulse. God had something in mind. As in the movie *Field of Dreams,* there was health and healing at hand.

Recall, Bruce was ready for a major career change. After twenty-six years with GE, he felt unchallenged. I was burned out in counseling, and we both were fed up with the nightly news (blues). We knew there was much more positive news to write about. The media just wasn't covering it. But there were also deeper, more personal reasons we wanted to escape suburbia.

I had been estranged from my children, Charlie and Katie, for a number of years, and that sorrow was catching up with me. I had too much of my own pain to counsel others effectively. Gathering stories of hope would at least help me face tomorrow. That's why stories about reunited families made my weary heart sing.

Two years on the road and into our upbeat news project, we visited Maggie and Reg Green at their home in Bodega Bay, California. Remember, the Greens lost their son, Nicholas. The seven-year-old was killed by a bandit's bullet while the family was vacationing in Italy (1994). The Green's miraculous decision to donate Nicholas' organs to seven Italians—a profound act of hope—helped them, over time, to bear the pain of losing their son.

While saying goodbye, Maggie asked Bruce and me if we had children. Bruce rattled off the names, ages, and independent status of his three grown children. I stumbled internally, then squeezed out a nondisclosing answer. "My daughter, Katie, is seventeen. She lives with her dad. My son, Charlie, is twenty. He goes to Dartmouth College," I said.

I couldn't say I hadn't seen my children in six years. I couldn't say how much I missed them. It wasn't right to lay my burdens, the result of divorce, on Maggie, who had ample sorrow of her own. I chose the silence of a counselor, though my pain jammed like a bone in my throat.

Thank God we were finished with the interview. As I climbed into our pickup truck, my life flashed before me—why I wanted out of Cleveland, why I couldn't listen to another sad story. What I could repress no longer was surfacing. For the longest time, I couldn't cry. Now I thought I'd never stop.

Not long after our visit with the Greens, I had a dream, and in the dream I was guided to write a letter to my son. I was to write out the words to the songs I sang to him when he was an infant. This simple exercise reminded me that even under extremely difficult circumstances and with an anguished heart, one is able to rejoice, give thanks, and sing.

So I wrote: *You are my sunshine, my only sunshine. A dream is a wish your heart makes, when you're fast asleep. I'm a Yankee Doodle Dandy. Swing low, sweet chariot coming for to carry me home.* And on and on.

Charlie Fiordalis, 22, and his mom, Julie Madsen. They had been separated for seven years.

In July, I received a phone call from Charlie. We talked, nonstop, for three short hours about his college classes and dream of being a writer, his relationship with his dad and stepmother, his pain of being separated from me for so long, and his hopes for the future. Our relationship was on the mend. Bruce and I traveled to New Hampshire that fall to see him. In November, Charlie came to California to visit us, and that Christmas (1997), on December 24, Katie called me from Ohio.

In January 1998, another miracle happened. Out of the blue, which I have come to believe means out of heaven, I received a call from the manager of an RV show in Michigan wanting me to do a seminar on "The Joys of RV Living," my ticket back East to see my daughter.

Katie Fiordalis, 20, and her mom, Julie Madsen are reunited after seven and one-half years.

After five days of seminar work, I rented a car and drove to Miami of Ohio's campus in Oxford. Katie was to meet me after her 4 P.M. class. I parked near her dorm at 4:55 P.M. and sat there, teary-eyed, waiting. Would I recognize my own child? Would all those years of sorrow break loose and drown both of us?

As if called by an angel, I glanced up at the second floor window of her dormitory and saw two young ladies sitting like mourning doves on the sill. Instantly, I knew which one was mine. I got out of the car and began walking toward the dorm. Seconds later, the door to Porter Hall flew open, and my beautiful grown daughter came running across the yard. I started running too. It was like an Irish Spring soap commercial—in slow motion two people who love each other jump into each other's arms and twirl around. The ice was broken and the frozen past, like the Wicked Witch of the West, was melting.

In June, Bruce, Katie, and I attended Charlie's graduation from Dartmouth College, one of the happiest days of my life. In September, I flew back East to take Katie to the University of Vermont, the school she was transferring to.

The joy continues. On Christmas Day, 1998, Katie was reunited with my family in Ohio. My parents hadn't seen the blonde-haired, blue-eyed princess in eight years!

And there's more. Remember, in the story "Joshua's Family," how Bruce's son Josh found his birth mother in the summer of 1998. On Christmas Eve, Bruce and I were honored guests at the Harris family reunion. Grace, Joshua's birth mother, thanked Bruce for raising Joshua in a good home. And Bruce expressed his gratitude by bringing Grace an album of pictures of Josh at different ages. Now Bruce boasts that he got to hug his son's mother for the first time.

Bruce Madsen, Joshua's birthmom Grace Harris, and Ruby Harris, Joshua's grandmother. Grace and Ruby and Joshua were separated since his birth.

In 1995, there were a few people who challenged our decision to leave all that we knew in search of upbeat news. "You can find it in your own backyard," they said. But something deeper was calling. Wherever a dream leads you, follow it. For us, it was across fifty states after which we were brought full circle back into our own lives, at a deeper level of appreciation. Remember, America was built on the dreams of pilgrims and pioneers. It is our heritage, and there is something very sacred about that.

The Rig: A 1995 Ford F-150 truck carried the Madsens and their 26-foot home-on-wheels, a 1995 SunnyBrook travel trailer, on their three-year odyssey.

Post Script

Often the post script is the most important part of a letter. In this case, it's the most important part of this book. Though INNER VIEWS: *Stories on the Strength of America* was written from a first person point of view, truly this was a collaborative effort. I could not and would not have gone on this journey, written this book, or experienced the beauty of this country and of the hundreds of fine people we met who make America great had it not been for the love and support of my husband, Bruce. He snapped the photos, arranged the ever-changing itinerary, was in constant contact with our publicist, Joyce Penhallurick, and the media, managed the business end of this three-year odyssey, published a bi-monthly newsletter, wrote a column for Chase Manhattan's RV website, fixed computer problems, and coped with all of the technical difficulties that accompany creating a mobile news room. Also, because I'm not confident with trucks and big rigs, he drove over 150,000 miles. But even deeper, I believe that because Bruce is a man of faith, we received the guidance we needed to allow us to bring our dream of getting more upbeat stories in the news, from heaven to earth.

J.M.

Julie Madsen, Ph.D., grew up in the Midwest. She began her career as a registered nurse, working in psychiatry and public health. For several years, she was a human resource specialist in a major hospital in Cleveland, Ohio, caring for the well-being of nurses. After earning a doctorate in counseling psychology, focusing on helping people choose meaningful work, she spent seven years in private counseling practice before embarking upon an adventurous writing career—her opportunity to promote health-boosting news.

Bruce Madsen, a native Californian, graduated from California Polytechnic and Stanford University before joining General Electric Company. His career at GE included manufacturing, education, and computer systems. Bruce also nurtured a parallel career—more than twenty years of single parenting three African-American children. He says that his children have been his greatest teachers, empowering him to search for life's deeper meaning. Since his marriage to Julie, the search continues through traveling the U.S., meeting people rich in diversity, and photojournaling their adventures as news.

The Madsens currently live in Sierra City, California.

To reach the Madsens . . .

If you have a story to share, call us at 1-800-714-1838, and we will return your call. You can e-mail us at madsenb@aol.com.

A subscription to our bi-monthy **INNER VIEWS** newsletter is $12 for 6 issues/year.

To order additional copies of **INNER VIEWS: Stories on the Strength of America,** please send check or money order for $14.95 plus $3.50 shipping , $1 shipping for each additional copy to:

Self Expression News Service
P. O. Box 451
Sierra City CA 96125-0451
California residents, add 7.25% tax, or $1.08 per book.

To order by phone, call toll-free, 1-800-714-1838. Use your MasterCard, Visa, Discover, or American Express card.